Finding Frassati

Christine M. Wohar

Finding Frassati
and Following His Path to Holiness

Foreword by Rt. Rev. Philip A. Egan,
Bishop of Portsmouth

EWTN PUBLISHING, INC.
Irondale, Alabama

EWTN Publishing, Inc.
5817 Old Leeds Road, Irondale, AL 35210

Distributed by Sophia Institute Press, Box 5284, Manchester, NH 03108.

paperback ISBN 978-1-68278-249-1
ebook ISBN 978-1-68278-250-7
Library of Congress Control Number: 2021938706

First printing

To Father John Sims Baker,
who introduced me to Blessed Frassati,
and to Wanda Gawronska,
who made it possible for me to get to know him so well:
thank you.

It would be an outrage to the memory of
Pier Giorgio to be enthusiastic about him without
attempting to model ourselves on his example.

—Baldovino di Rovasenda

Contents

Foreword

Blessed Pier Giorgio Frassati (1901–1925) is surely one of the most fascinating saints of our time. Born in an era close enough to our own as to be very familiar, he grew up in a world of industry, education, media, and travel, with all the challenges young people face today. He came from a wealthy and well-connected family. His mother was an artist and a great influence on him. His father was the founder and owner of an Italian daily newspaper, *La Stampa*, and was a diplomat and one-time ambassador to Germany. A young man of film-star looks, Pier Giorgio had a lively, enthralling personality. Fit and strongly athletic, he loved cycling, skiing, swimming, horseback riding, and, above all, mountain climbing. As a university student, he did his best with his studies but found them constantly a struggle. He was the life and soul of a group of close friends, an association he founded called the *Tipi Loschi* (the "Shady Ones"). Relishing their company and earning their deep loyalty and affection, he enjoyed a drink, smoked an occasional cigar, played practical jokes, debated politics, and fell in love. His life was an avalanche of energy, but a life cut short, unexpectedly, at the age of twenty-four.

What in part helps to make Blessed Pier Giorgio so fascinating is that we know such a lot about him, so many personal details, thanks to his younger sister, Luciana, with whom he was very close. After his death, she wrote several books and published collections of the family photographs. Many who knew Pier Giorgio also recorded their stories and personal impressions. A family friend who was an artist depicted him in paintings. A lot of short testimonies about his faith, his charity, and his commitment to social justice have survived from those who knew him or had met him. Above all, we have many of the letters he wrote from childhood to adulthood. These give us a deep insight into his daily life and concerns, his intimate thoughts and feelings. As he grew up and faced life's ups and downs, these letters disclose his soul. More fascinating still, they clearly reveal the hand of God, the working of God's grace, the growing aroma of God's love.

Finally, what is most fascinating about Pier Giorgio is the intensity of his faith. Secretly in the slums, he gave away his wealth and much of his spare time serving the poor as a member of the St. Vincent de Paul Society: *I see a special light around the sick, the poor, the less fortunate, a light we do not possess,* he said. He was passionate about justice, economics, and politics, an advocate of authentic Catholic social teaching. Early every morning, he went to Mass: *Jesus comes to me each day in Holy Communion and I return the visit by going to serve the poor.* He often took part in nocturnal Eucharistic Adoration. People saw a radiance in his face, in his joy, and in his purity. Like other saints, he had an intense love for Jesus in the Eucharist and an intense love for Jesus in the poor. It was in the slums, or more likely in his hospital work, that he caught polio and died after an agonizing illness of just six days. To the amazement of his family, who knew little of his inner life, great crowds of the urban poor turned out for the funeral.

In recent times, Blessed Pier Giorgio Frassati has been recommended to the Church by Pope Saint John Paul II, Pope Benedict XVI, and Pope Francis. An ordinary Christian, he was extraordinary, the "Man of the Beatitudes." A model of Christian youth, he is a patron of World Youth Day, Catholic sports clubs, and countless youth associations. He certainly deserves to be better known in the English-speaking world. We should all get to know him. Unfortunately, although there are many books about him in Italian, some of his sister's main works have not yet been translated. We have so much more to learn from his faith, his words, and his inspiring example. In this regard, we are all deeply grateful to Pier Giorgio's wonderful niece, Wanda Gawronska, for her lifelong efforts to perpetuate his legacy.

We should also be grateful to Christine Wohar, founder of FrassatiUSA, for this book, *Finding Frassati and Following His Path to Holiness*. Not only is having a new book in English a great joy for English-speaking audiences; it adds further detail, some further brush strokes, if you like, to our picture of Pier Giorgio. Wohar writes in a simple, accessible style, in short reflections that can easily be used as part of our daily prayer. She presents biographical details, testimonies, and extracts from Pier Giorgio's letters and sayings, some for the first time in English. But more than that, this is a book that can help us put his spirituality into practice through prayer and action. Wohar challenges us, as disciples of Christ, to grow in faith and holiness, taking inspiration from the example of Blessed Frassati himself. It is just the sort of book we need.

Friendship with the saints is a personal affair. I always believe it's the saints who choose and befriend us, not the other way round. I thank Blessed Pier Giorgio for his love and friendship, for enlisting me among his worldwide *Tipi Loschi*, and for encouraging me to reach *verso l'alto*, "to the heights" — to the Lord Jesus and the happiness and holiness He calls us to. I thank Giorgio, too, for his powerful intercession and for obtaining so many answers to my prayers.

With the help of this fine book, may you also, through his intercession, receive the answers to your prayers.

—Rt. Rev. Philip A. Egan BA, STL, PhD
Bishop of Portsmouth (UK)

An Opening Note

I was first introduced to Blessed Pier Giorgio Frassati about five years after his beatification. I had just moved to Nashville, Tennessee, to attend law school, and a priest at my new parish asked me to help him start a group for young adults. He decided to call it the Frassati Society. I knew absolutely nothing about this Frassati.

In time, I would discover that Pier Giorgio Frassati and I had a lot in common: an Italian heritage, a grandmother named Josephine, a love for coffee, the beach, music, practical jokes, horseback riding, languages. He was light-years ahead of me in his spiritual practices, however, although I share many of them now. Many of them I still struggle with, such as his selfless apostolate of charity.

When I met his niece Wanda, his sister Luciana, and other members of his family in 2006, I knew the path of my life was about to take a wild detour to an unknown destination. And so it has. Blessed Pier Giorgio Frassati has journeyed with me every step of the way, as faithful a friend as one could ever hope to know.

Toward the end of a newspaper article published shortly after Pier Giorgio's death in 1925, the president of the Catholic university club for men in Turin wrote, "It would be an outrage to the memory of Pier Giorgio to be enthusiastic about him without attempting to model ourselves on his example." I wholeheartedly agree. My hope is that the simple reflections in this book will inspire you to be enthusiastic about him *and* follow his example.

I am so grateful to have found him, and I am glad that you have too.

Verso l'alto!

A Brief Biography of Blessed Pier Giorgio Frassati

Pier Giorgio Michelangelo Frassati was born in Turin, Italy, on April 6, 1901. His mother, Adelaide Ametis, was a talented artist. His father, Alfredo, was the founder and director of the newspaper *La Stampa* and was influential in Italian politics, holding positions as an Italian senator and ambassador to Germany. At an early age, Pier Giorgio joined the Marian Sodality and the Apostleship of Prayer and obtained permission to receive daily Communion (which was rare at that time). He developed a deep spiritual life, which he never hesitated to share with his friends. The Holy Eucharist and the Blessed Virgin were the two anchors of his world of prayer. At the age of seventeen, he joined the St. Vincent de Paul Society and dedicated much of his spare time to serving the sick and the needy.

He decided to become a mining engineer so he could "*serve Christ better among the miners*," as he told a friend. Although he considered his studies his first duty, they did not keep him from social and political activism. In 1919, he joined the organization known as Catholic Action. He became a very active member of the People's Party, which promoted the Catholic Church's social teaching based on the principles of Pope Leo XIII's encyclical letter *Rerum Novarum*.

Finding Frassati

What little he did have Pier Giorgio gave to help the poor, even using his bus fare for charity and then running home to be on time for meals. His charity involved not simply giving something to others but giving completely of himself. This love of neighbor was fed by daily communion with Christ in the Holy Eucharist, frequent nocturnal Adoration of the Blessed Sacrament, and meditation on Saint Paul's "Hymn of Charity" (1 Cor. 13). He often sacrificed vacations at the Frassati summer home in Pollone (outside Turin) because, as he said, "*If everybody leaves Turin, who will take care of the poor?*"

In 1921, he was a central figure in Ravenna, enthusiastically helping to organize the first convention of Pax Romana, an association that had as its aim the unification of all Catholic students throughout the world for the purpose of working together for universal peace.

Mountain climbing was one of Pier Giorgio's favorite sports. Outings in the mountains, which he organized with his friends, also served as opportunities for his apostolic work. He never lost the chance to lead his friends to Mass, to the reading of Scripture, and to praying the Rosary. He often went to the theater, to the opera, and to museums. He loved art and music and could quote whole passages of the poet Dante.

Fondness for the epistles of Saint Paul sparked his zeal for fraternal charity. The fiery sermons of the Renaissance preacher and reformer Girolamo Savonarola and the writings of Saint Catherine of Siena impelled him in 1922 to join the Lay Dominicans (the Third Order of Saint Dominic). He chose the name Girolamo after his personal hero, Savonarola. "*I am a fervent admirer of this friar, who died as a saint at the stake,*" he wrote to a friend.

Like his father, he was strongly anti-Fascist and did nothing to hide his political views. On occasion, he even physically defended the Faith in fights with anti-clerical Communists and later with Fascists who violently entered his family's home.

Just before receiving his university degree, Pier Giorgio contracted poliomyelitis, which doctors later speculated he caught from the sick whom he tended. Because his grandmother was dying, he did not call attention to his own failing health. After several days of terrible suffering, he died at the age of twenty-four on July 4, 1925.

His last preoccupation was for the poor. On the eve of his death, with a paralyzed hand, he scribbled a message to a friend, asking him to take the medicine needed for injections to a poor sick man he had been visiting.

Pier Giorgio's funeral was a triumph. The streets of the city were lined with a multitude of mourners who were unknown to his family: the poor and the needy whom he had served so unselfishly for seven years. Many of these people, in turn, were surprised to learn that the saintly young man they knew had been the heir of the influential Frassati family.

Pope Saint John Paul II, after visiting the original tomb of Pier Giorgio in the family plot in Pollone, said in 1989: "I wanted to pay homage to a young man who was able to witness to Christ with singular effectiveness in this century of ours. When I was a young man, I, too, felt the beneficial influence of his example, and, as a student, I was impressed by the force of his testimony."[1]

On May 20, 1990, in St. Peter's Square, which was filled with thousands of people, the pope beatified Pier Giorgio Frassati, calling him the "man of the eight beatitudes."[2]

After his beatification, his mortal remains, found completely intact and incorrupt upon their exhumation on March 31, 1981, were transferred from the family tomb in Pollone to the cathedral

---

[1] Quoted in Luciana Frassati, *A Man of the Beatitudes: Pier Giorgio Frassati* (San Francisco: Ignatius Press, 2000), 172.

[2] "Why Was Blessed Pier Giorgio Called 'The Man of the Beatitudes'?" FrassatiUSA, https://frassatiusa.org/man-of-the-beatitudes.

in Turin. Many pilgrims, especially students and the young, visit the resting place of Blessed Frassati to seek favors and the courage to follow his example.[3]

[3] Adapted from the brief biography at FrassatiUSA, https://frassatiusa. org/frassati-biography. See also Luciana Frassati, *A Man of the Beatitudes* (San Francisco: Ignatius Press, 2001), 9–13.

1

A Transatlantic Leap of Faith

I am happy because my sister is happy.[4]

Was I dreaming? No, it was actually the voice of Luciana Frassati coming from the grand staircase just outside my bedroom door.

"Ventidue ... ventitre ... ventiquattro ..." She was counting the number of steps as she carefully descended each one with the help of a young aide on her way to breakfast in the room adjacent to the dining room where she often took her meals.

This, I came to learn over the next several weeks, was the morning routine for the 104-year-old sister of Blessed Pier Giorgio Frassati. And there I was, an obscure American, living in the house with her.

The five-floor country residence known as the Villa Ametis — built by Francesco Ametis, the maternal grandfather of Pier Giorgio and Luciana — was the home away from home for the family throughout their lives. They made so many memories there, and now I was making precious ones of my own. Hearing Luciana's voice in the morning, sitting with her on the veranda, sharing a

---

[4] Pier Giorgio Frassati, *Letters to His Friends and Family* (Staten Island, NY: St. Paul's/Alba House, 2009), 203.

meal with her: those were priceless moments when I felt very close to Pier Giorgio.

How do you wake up in Nashville, Tennessee, one morning and in Pollone, Italy, the next? By taking a giant leap of faith. I am not the first person to walk away from a professional career to do something a little nontraditional; but this was pretty far outside my comfort zone and quite surreal on a daily basis.

Although she had been fluent in several languages, Luciana spoke mostly Italian and Polish in her final years. One day, however, she began a conversation with me in English. She asked if my room was comfortable and told me how important it was to do the work on behalf of Pier Giorgio. It was a brief exchange and one I will never forget.

The following year, I enjoyed a few more weeks in her presence. She died after a brief illness in the home where she had been born. Because of providential circumstances, I was blessed to attend her funeral. Flying back to the United States the next day, I felt an even greater sense of responsibility for helping to carry on the work Luciana had begun. And I had the feeling that she would be watching over me.

At some point, discernment of God's will has to lead to action. One thing I've learned in the great adventure of life: when you take a leap of faith, you may land in some amazing places.

Pray

Heavenly Father,
Give me the courage to strive for the highest goals,
to flee every temptation to be mediocre.
Enable me to aspire to greatness, as Pier Giorgio did,
and to open my heart with joy to Your call to holiness.

Free me from the fear of failure.
I want to be firmly and forever united to You, Lord.
Grant me the graces I ask You
through Pier Giorgio's intercession,
by the merits of Our Lord Jesus Christ.
Amen.

Act

Is the Lord calling you to serve Him in a different way? Have you been reluctant to respond? Pray the above prayer for courage to take the next right step.

2

Nicknames and No Names

Dear wonderful daddy, I love you so much so that you will be happy I will not hit Luciana anymore. Happy feastday—I will pray to Baby Jesus for you. He kisses you—your Dodo.[5]

Growing up with nine brothers and sisters, it was not uncommon for our parents to confuse our names every now and then. When they would load us into the station wagon for a road trip, it was an amusing custom for my dad to call roll to be sure everyone was in the car. I remember quite well the time my brother Greg didn't answer; we were already on the road on our way home, and we had to turn around and anxiously search for him. Was that how it was for Joseph and Mary when they lost track of twelve-year-old Jesus? We found Greg on the beach, playing contentedly in the sand—not at all aware that we had been miles down the road without him.

For some reason, my brother Steve was always getting new nicknames, such as Spud, Riggs, Punky, and DeBoy. There was a boy on our street we called Coco, and I honestly do not know what his real name was. My name gets a lot of variations: Chrissy and Chris and Christina, with the occasional inside-joke nicknames of

[5] Frassati, *Letters*, 1.

X and Clisti. It's gotten so that when people ask what to call me, I really don't know what to tell them anymore and usually just say, "Take your pick."

Pier Giorgio Frassati was not a stranger to nicknames. In fact, he liked to give them to himself and his friends. As a small child, he called himself Dodo. In later years, he and his best friend, Marco Beltramo, became Robespierre and Perrault, jokingly making up the "terror subsection" of the Tipi Loschi.[6] His friend Franz he called Petronius because of his stylish dress; Ernestina was changed to Englesina after a trip to London. With his creative sense of humor, no wonder his friends loved being in his presence!

Despite his fun with nicknames, the one name *never* used for Pier Giorgio was Pier. Nobody called him that because such a name does not exist in Italian. Pier is a shortened form of Pietro that is only used when followed by another name, as in Pier Giorgio. If his friends or family shortened his name, they would use Giorgio. I often question the credibility of the source when I see him referred to as "Pier" in articles, social media posts, videos, and so forth, although I suppose it happens quite innocently. Anyone seeing the name Pier Giorgio Frassati might reasonably—but wrongly—think that Giorgio is his middle name (which is actually Michelangelo).

It may seem trivial and not worth this long explanation to some. But getting someone's name right is important—especially to that person. In the case of Blessed Pier Giorgio Frassati, it is essential. There are so many options: Pier Giorgio Frassati, Giorgio Frassati, Blessed Frassati, Blessed Pier Giorgio Frassati, Blessed Giorgio Frassati, Pier Giorgio Michelangelo Frassati, Pier Giorgio, Giorgio—to name more than a few! And, God willing, someday soon, Saint Frassati will be on that list. But never, never, never Pier.

---

[6] The Tipi Loschi Society was a group of Pier Giorgio's closest friends who shared many adventures and, above all, a spiritual bond.

Pray

O Father, You gave to the young Pier Giorgio Frassati the joy of meeting Christ and of living his faith in the service of the poor and the sick; through his intercession may we, too, walk the path of the Beatitudes and follow the example of his generosity, spreading the spirit of the gospel in society. Through Christ our Lord. Amen.

— +Cardinal Giovanni Saldarini, Archbishop of Turin

Act

Write "Never Pier" one hundred times. Just kidding. But please never say it!

3

The Pool-Playing Saint

*I am here by myself, so I rarely take walks; only the Marchisios
are here, with whom I play billiards some evenings.*[7]

❖

The image of Pier Giorgio Frassati leaning over a pool table with
a cue stick in his hand is probably not the first one that comes to
mind when people think of him. Because of his spiritual depth, it's
easy to forget that he was just a normal guy who enjoyed spending
time with his friends on campus.

Mingled within the pages of his book of letters is a somewhat
amusing episode from his student life. At the Regio Politecnico
(Royal Polytechnic) of Turin, where he was majoring in mining
engineering, Pier Giorgio belonged to a Catholic club for young
men. Playing pool with fellow members was an activity that he
enjoyed. When the condition of their table deteriorated and they
could no longer play, something had to be done.

Pier Giorgio took it upon himself to go to a repair shop, where
the owner agreed to fix the table and give them new cue sticks,
balls, and a new cue-stick holder for the sum of 1,500 lire. Four
months later, Pier Giorgio was in Berlin and learned that the man

[7] Frassati, *Letters*, 17.

had still not delivered what he promised. He sent a letter to his friend Antonio Severi: "*I'm hurrying to answer you because it's about something urgent. Mr. DeAgostini really doesn't keep his word and I'm not surprised, because, as soon as our contract was signed, I heard bad things about him, but I didn't really believe that he would go this far.*"[8]

Apparently, Mr. DeAgostini was demanding more money to do what he had agreed to earlier. Pier Giorgio's next sentence may seem out of character to those who only think of his saintly ways. Not only did he suggest writing a fiery letter, but he instructed Antonio "*not to pay him for the moment and to wait for me to arrive in Italy, and then I'll go and find Mr. DeAgostini and tell him off.*"

Two months later, Pier Giorgio returned from Germany. The contract dispute was still on his mind. Did he find Mr. DeAgostini and tell him off? Unlikely. The pool table was eventually repaired and restored to the club after new terms were negotiated for a slightly higher amount.

When I first read about the pool-table ordeal, it struck me as so out of character for Pier Giorgio to react so strongly about something so minor in comparison with all of the weighty political and social issues he faced. Of course, I should have known he had an underlying higher motive, which was revealed in another of his letters: having a billiards room at the university club meant that the guys would stay on campus to enjoy quality fellowship rather than going out to play in pool rooms or in the bars of Turin, where he feared their morals would be corrupted.

Stories have circulated over the years about Pier Giorgio's practice of making a friendly wager over a game of billiards. If he won, the loser would pay up by attending Eucharistic Adoration or going to Mass or doing some other spiritual activity that would benefit his soul. Being able to evangelize his friends in this subtle

---

[8] Frassati, *Letters*, 103.

way is another reason why it was so important for Pier Giorgio to have the club's pool table repaired as quickly as possible. Of course, there is a third reason we shouldn't overlook: he just liked to play!

Pray

Blessed Pier Giorgio, most Christian
of companions, pray for us!

Act

Do you have a friend or relative who hasn't been to church for some time? Think of a fun wager you can make to help that person find his or her way back. Be sure to win!

4

Mountains, Mountains, Mountains, I Love You!

If my studies would allow me to do it, I would
spend entire days on the mountains contemplating
in that pure air the Greatness of the Creator.[9]

The arguably most famous three words in mountaineering are at-tributed to a young pipe-smoking alpinist who was considered one of the best of his time. When asked why he wanted to climb Mount Everest, George Mallory answered, "Because it's there." He died on its north face in 1924, and his body was discovered seventy-five years later.

Another young pipe-smoking alpinist used five words to de-scribe his climbing motivation: *"to feel that pure joy."* Like George Mallory, Giorgio Frassati was well aware of the risks one took in going into the mountains. It wasn't uncommon for him to take out a life-insurance policy before undertaking a particularly chal-lenging climb.

He reflected on the risk-reward aspect of his passion for the mountains in a letter to a friend. The president of the Catholic mountaineering association had recently fallen to his death before

[9] Frassati, *Letters*, 132.

his sister's eyes on the Chateau des Dames—a peak Pier Giorgio had scaled without any trouble two years earlier. Contemplating this, he wrote: "*And so the moral is: when one goes into the mountains one should sort out one's conscience first, because one never knows if one will return. But despite all this I'm not afraid and on the contrary I want to climb the mountains more than ever, to conquer the most daring peaks; to feel that pure joy, which one can only have in the mountains.*"[10]

From early childhood, Pier Giorgio was accustomed to going on long excursions with family and friends. He could gaze at the peak of Mount Mucrone from his bedroom window at the summer home in Pollone. Mountain ranges provided the backdrop for his hometown of Turin. It's no wonder that he wrote, "*Every day that goes by I fall deeply in love with the mountains; their charm attracts me.*"[11]

During one of my stays in Pollone, I was able to climb nearby Mount Camino with the help of a young French priest. Having grown up around mountains, Père Marc could practically leap from rock to rock. It was a humbling experience for me to have to take his hand so often on the descent when my knees reached their limit of endurance. Even a climb as simple (for some) and straightforward as the hike to the top of Mount Camino can give you a taste of that pure joy Pier Giorgio said he had only in the mountains. In those mountains, his mountains, you are beckoned by the same spirit that led him higher and higher in a quest to hear the voice of God better. Carefully seeking footing on the way down, you are reminded that, just as in the spiritual life, one wrong step can have serious consequences.

Notwithstanding the cavalier quote he is known for, it's safe to say that George Mallory was drawn to the mountains for many other reasons. After all, the mountains are more than just there.

[10] Frassati, *Letters*, 134.
[11] Frassati, *Letters*, 128.

Finding Frassati

They are more even than a metaphor for life. They are classrooms of contemplation of the Creator. In this, Giorgio Frassati was one of the best students of his time. And probably ours.

---------⊛---------

Pray

Blessed Frassati, conqueror of life's mountains, pray for us!

---------⊛---------

Act

Take a slow walk and try to appreciate the beauty of creation all around you.

5

The Waters of Baptism

And let us hope that this Faith that we have
received in Holy Baptism ... will accompany us
until the last day of our earthly journey.[12]

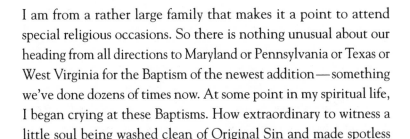

I am from a rather large family that makes it a point to attend special religious occasions. So there is nothing unusual about our heading from all directions to Maryland or Pennsylvania or Texas or West Virginia for the Baptism of the newest addition — something we've done dozens of times now. At some point in my spiritual life, I began crying at these Baptisms. How extraordinary to witness a little soul being washed clean of Original Sin and made spotless in the sight of God. Tears of joy are called for!

Pier Giorgio's Baptism was not as joyful an occasion for his family because of the circumstances. He was born with third-degree asphyxiation, so they had to call for the priest and do it quickly without an elaborate ceremony. The rite was not completed until five months later with godparents present. Maybe that double dose of grace is what made Pier Giorgio so special!

[12] Frassati, *Letters,* 167.

Finding Frassati

Throughout his life, Pier Giorgio was always finding ways to lead others to the sacraments. Whether it was Baptism or Penance or Holy Communion or even the Anointing of the Sick, he wanted people to take advantage of the graces available to them.

In one case, he even served as godfather for a baby of a poor family. When he learned that the mother was putting off the Baptism because she did not have money for a baptismal gown, he provided the funds and encouraged her to do it quickly. He mentioned his participation in the ceremony very casually in a letter to a friend: *"Now I have a goddaughter, who is 20 days old, I held her at the baptism the other day; she is pretty enough as far as babies are; at that age they're more or less all the same."*[13]

In his own life, Pier Giorgio acknowledged how much strength he drew from the sacraments — especially when going through personal turmoil. Like us, he experienced doubts and uncertainties, but he never let them lead him away from God. As he was coming to the end of his university days, he questioned the direction of his life in a letter to a friend: *"Every now and then I ask myself: shall I go on trying to follow the right path? Will I have the good fortune to persevere to the end? In this tremendous clash of doubts, the Faith given to me in Baptism suggests to me with a sure voice: 'By yourself you can do nothing, but if you have God as the center of your every action then, yes, you will reach the goal.'"*[14]

As the catechism teaches, each sacrament is an outward sign instituted by God to give us grace. In other words, each sacrament in some way strengthens our connection with God and keeps Him at the center of all we do. Without the sacraments, we become spiritual drifters.

[13] Frassati, *Letters*, 140.
[14] Frassati, *Letters*, 197.

Pier Giorgio set his sights on the summit of both earthly and spiritual mountains. He understood that, in both situations, having the proper tools was necessary to succeed. On his spiritual climb, the tools he carried were the sacraments. They certainly worked well because he made it to the top. Now he beckons us to use them on our journey *verso l'alto*.

Pray
ACT OF FAITH

O my God, I firmly believe that You are one God in three
divine Persons, Father, Son, and Holy Spirit. I believe
that Your divine Son became man and died for our
sins and that He will come to judge the living and the
dead. I believe these and all the truths which the holy
Catholic Church teaches, because You have revealed
them, Who can neither deceive nor be deceived. Amen.

Act

Do you know the date of your Baptism? Put it on your calendar and celebrate it.

6

Pier Giorgio's Eucharistic Life

*Jesus Christ has promised to those who feed
themselves with the most Holy Eucharist, eternal
life and the necessary graces to obtain it.*[15]

———————— ❁ ————————

Have you ever attended a Eucharistic Congress? It is a thing of true beauty to attend the closing Mass and see a great procession of bishops, priests, deacons, seminarians, and altar servers making its way through a gathering of thousands of lay faithful — all for Jesus in the Eucharist.

Pier Giorgio made it a point to participate in Eucharistic Congresses when possible. On April 2, 1922, he sent a postcard to his mother with just one sentence: "*A thousand greetings and kisses from the Eucharistic Congress.*"[16] The following year, he rearranged his schedule so that he could attend a Eucharistic Congress in Genoa, where an amazing procession of the Blessed Sacrament took place both on sea and on land. Although these occasional large events filled him with enthusiasm, it was a regular appointment on his

---

[15] Frassati, *Letters*, 129.
[16] Frassati, *Letters*, 82.

calendar that fortified his soul: his daily meeting with Jesus in Holy Communion.

Pier Giorgio was ten years old when he made his First Holy Communion, on June 19, 1911. In those days, he would have had to wait until he turned twelve; Pope Pius X issued a decree in the summer of 1910, however, that allowed children to receive the Sacrament at "the age of reason"—about seven years old.[17] The papal decree did even more than lower the age of First Communion; it also urged parents to enable their children to receive frequently, even daily, if possible.

This opportunity presented itself to Pier Giorgio two years later, when, at age twelve, he was enrolled in a school operated by the Jesuit Fathers. There he was encouraged by the headmaster, and obtained permission from his mother, to begin receiving Our Lord daily in the Blessed Sacrament. For the next twelve years, the Eucharist became the central point of Pier Giorgio's life and the driving force behind his works of charity. *"Jesus comes to me every day in Holy Communion,"* he said. *"I repay him in my miserable way by visiting the poor."*[18] He received the Eucharist for the last time on his deathbed, on July 3, 1925—a mere fourteen years after making his First Holy Communion.

It has been said that if we truly believed in the Real Presence, we would go crawling on our hands and knees to receive the Eucharist. Pier Giorgio believed. The effort he made as a teenager and young adult to receive daily Communion is even more impressive when you consider that his mother went to Church only on Sundays and his father was a fallen-away Catholic who did not attend Mass with the family.

---

[17] Pope Pius X, *Quam Singulari* (August 15, 1910), a decree on admitting children to the Eucharist.

[18] Luciana Frassati, *Mio Fratello Pier Giorgio: La Fede* (Rome: Figlie di San Paolo, 2004), 301.

Speaking to Catholic youth in his area, Pier Giorgio appealed to them with all the strength of his soul to *"become totally consumed by this Eucharistic Fire."*[19] By doing so, he said, they would find the strength to fight interior temptations and gain all of the necessary graces to obtain eternal life with Christ and true happiness on earth. These weren't mere words. Pier Giorgio lived them. His example challenges us to do the same.

❧

Pray

I do believe, help my unbelief! (Mark 9:24)

❧

Act

Inspired by the example of Blessed Frassati, let us take advantage of every opportunity to receive Our Lord worthily in the Eucharist and encourage others to do the same. Go to an extra Mass this week and, if possible, bring a friend.

---

[19] Frassati, *Letters*, 129.

7

Pushed Around by the Holy Spirit

*We Catholics must strive to have our whole
life guided by Christian moral law.* [20]

On June 10, 1915, Pier Giorgio and his sister Luciana received
the Sacrament of Confirmation together at their parish church in
Turin. He was fourteen, and she was approaching thirteen. (Because
they were just sixteen months apart, Mrs. Frassati had chosen to
raise them almost like twins, to be a support and protection for
each other in life.)

Luciana retained no spiritual recollections about the day. Based
on her research, the only person in the Frassati household who
could give any insight into Pier Giorgio's reaction was the family
cook. Although eleven years had gone by, she still remembered
asking Pier Giorgio, "What did you ask Him, what grace did you
request from the Lord today as you were confirmed?" He answered,
"*I asked for a grace for me and a grace for Luciana.*" He refused to
elaborate about what graces he specifically asked for because, as

[20] Frassati, *Letters*, 129.

he said, "*If you tell anyone what graces you asked for, the Lord won't grant them anymore.*"[21]

It is not possible to know for sure what was in Pier Giorgio's heart or mind on his Confirmation day, but the impact of the Holy Spirit on his life is impossible to miss. Charity, joy, peace, patience, kindness, goodness, long-suffering, mildness, faith, modesty, self-restraint, chastity: these twelve fruits of the Spirit were overflowing in him and rubbed off on all those fortunate enough to cross his path.

I'm reminded of another George who was filled with the Holy Spirit: a beloved priest from Nashville, who, until his death at age ninety-seven, still offered Mass for the residents at his assisted-living home. He was known for his pragmatic advice, candor, and gruff old voice. "Do! Say!" were the words I heard from the other side of the confessional screen on one occasion. "Can you remember those two words?" And then he explained, "When you get up in the morning, ask the Holy Spirit to push you around. Ask Him to only let you *do* or *say* the things you really should. Anything more would be pride, and anything less would be sloth. Do! Say! Got it?" I got it. I even wrote it down as soon as I got back to the pew to be sure I never forgot it.

It's easy to see how Pier Giorgio let the Holy Spirit push him around because nearly everything he did and said was impactful. He wasn't sinless, but he was striving to be. He was living and not merely existing. He was growing in virtue and bearing spiritual fruit until he drew his last breath. Even then, he had such a humble view of himself, writing: "*Surely Divine Providence in His Marvelous Plans sometimes uses us miserable little twigs to do Good.*"[22]

[21] L. Frassati, *Mio Fratello Pier Giorgio*, 59.
[22] Frassati, *Letters*, 224.

What a world this would be if we could all become "miserable little twigs" like Blessed Pier Giorgio Frassati! With the Holy Spirit pushing us around, we can. Do! Say! Got it?

Pray

Byzantine Catholic Prayer

Heavenly King, Comforter, Spirit of Truth,
Who is everywhere present and fills all things,
Treasury of Blessings and Giver of Life,
come and dwell within us,
cleanse us of all stain,
and save our souls,
O Gracious Lord. Amen.

Act

Ask the Holy Spirit to push you around today. Be open to His inspirations and willing to act on them.

8

Pier Giorgio's Practice of Penance

*In His Infinite Mercy, God has surely not
kept my innumerable sins in mind.*[23]

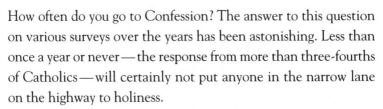

How often do you go to Confession? The answer to this question
on various surveys over the years has been astonishing. Less than
once a year or never—the response from more than three-fourths
of Catholics—will certainly not put anyone in the narrow lane
on the highway to holiness.

Consider that saints such as Mother Teresa and Pope John Paul
II went to Confession at least weekly. Blessed Pier Giorgio also went
very frequently—sometimes daily. Why? Did they know a secret
about this sacrament that is hidden from the rest of us?

One of my favorite stories is an account of a time when Pier
Giorgio went to Confession on a busy sidewalk in Turin. According
to a priest named Father Righini, they ran into each other one day
around 11:00 a.m. while crossing the street. Pier Giorgio was on
his way to Mass at La Consolata, a beautiful and beloved basilica.
After greeting the priest, Pier Giorgio asked if he "*could have the*

[23] Frassati, *Letters*, 137.

pleasure of going to confession." As Father Righini looked around for a nearby church, Pier Giorgio said, *"That's not necessary. I'll confess here on the street."* He removed his hat, made a large Sign of the Cross, and humbly began his confession.[24]

This type of encounter was out of the ordinary for Father Righini, who admitted to being very distracted while hearing the confession. He noted, though, that Pier Giorgio had no concern at all for what anyone passing by might have thought, and afterward, he went on his way satisfied and happy.

Pier Giorgio received the Sacrament of Confession for the first time on June 11, 1910. Over the years, as he came to believe that the smallest sin could lead to greater sins, he sought God's forgiveness for the most minor displays of impatience or annoyance. Luciana Frassati wrote that her brother "wanted to approach God more frequently to purify his soul, and he sought help from his confessor's advice so that he could live the Christian life more deeply. Possessing the Lord's peace, it was easier for him to suffer, to make sacrifices, to deal with the daily silence in our house and the harsh tests of charity outside the home."[25]

Perhaps, then, this was the secret known also by saints such as Mother Teresa and Pope John Paul II, who frequently confessed; that is, the regular practice of Confession fortifies us to endure the trials we face and to resist the near occasion of sin in our daily lives. Actually, this is not a secret. At some level, we all know it. We just tend to focus more attention on our sins than on the graces awaiting us in the confessional. Or, as the case may be, on the side of a busy street.

[24] L. Frassati, *Mio Fratello Pier Giorgio*, 36.
[25] L. Frassati, *Mio Fratello Pier Giorgio*, 28.

Pray

ACT OF CONTRITION

My God, I am sorry for my sins with all my heart.
In choosing to do wrong and failing to do good,
I have sinned against You, Whom I should love
above all things. I firmly intend, with Your help, to
do penance, to sin no more, and to avoid whatever
leads me to sin. Our Savior Jesus Christ suffered and
died for us. In His name, my God, have mercy.

Act

If you've been away from the sacraments for a while, ask
Blessed Pier Giorgio to help you make a good confession
this week. The spiritual lives of his friends were always a
priority for him, and he will not let you down.

9

Letters from the Sea

The beach is very beautiful, the sea is stupendous;
it only lacks warmth and so my swims have to
be very short. I'm already deep red.[26]

I crossed off another of my Frassati bucket-list items one summer
when I was finally able to visit Forte dei Marmi, an Italian coastal
town where the Frassati family often vacationed. The town takes
its name, supposedly, from the fortress (*forte*) there where marble
(*marmi*) was kept before being shipped. My visit was short — just
long enough to stroll through the open-air market and inhale a
few breaths of the sea.

Even though many with a devotion to Blessed Frassati think of
him as a mountain climber and skier, he was quite the beach bum.
As a child and teenager, he spent many summers visiting cousins in
Alassio, where he would fish, swim, and sail to his heart's content.
Another frequent beach spot was Albissola, where he wrote one
of my favorite letters to his mother, "*I'm here at Albissola; I arrived
in a pitiful condition, dirty as a pig.*"[27]

[26] Frassati, *Letters*, 24.
[27] Frassati, *Letters*, 29.

Finding Frassati

He spared his mother the details of his ninety-mile bike trip so she wouldn't worry, but he explained it all to his good friend Carlo in a separate letter:

> *Right after we parted I began to have accidents on the trip. At Ceriana . . . I had to fix the inner tube which went flat and so I wasted time until three. I was able to get to Savona from here in two hours, but right after Spotorno, a long way from town, my tire blew out again; so after failed attempts to repair it, I decided to take the bus to Vado. From there, having fixed the tire, I arrived in Albissola Superiore at 8:30.*[28]

What an ordeal! But he didn't seem to mind. Did he bike that distance with a backpack full of his beach gear, I wonder? Such an incredible athlete!

His last summer vacation, in August 1924, was spent in Forte dei Marmi. The many letters he wrote that summer—probably more were written than were retrieved and eventually published —paint such a personal portrait of his interests and what mattered in his life.

He set out on the trip after finally passing an exam in electrotechnology with the unimpressive score of 70. His letter to a friend detailing what he called the *"comic drama surrounding my exam"*[29] gives us an inside glimpse of his outlook on his academic life.

In more than one letter, he shares that he has a stack of books with him at the beach to study for his next exam in metallurgy but has way too many distractions. So relatable. In another letter, he shares his dream of skiing down the mountains in the winter completely free from all exams. You can sense his anguish and how much he longed to be finished with his studies.

[28] Frassati, *Letters*, 29.
[29] Frassati, *Letters*, 168.

He writes to his aunt, promising prayers for her feast day: "*I will pray a lot for you and I will receive Holy Communion for you and Luciana.*"[30]

He vents his frustration with the state of the Catholic political party and government in general: "*How can a party call itself Catholic, when it supports a government that has no morals namely when it has made the morals of assassins and robbers its own?*"[31]

The love for his friends comes to life in these beach letters, as well. He jokes with his friend Marco about their good friend Tina, who was away in England. He contemplates a visit to see Laura, to whom he was becoming strongly attracted. He describes the lunch he prepared for some friends during which he wore that now infamous paper hat.

He also writes one of his famous "proclamations" sending "a torpedo blast" rather than the usual cannon blast from the "terror section" of the Tipi Loschi. Although these proclamations were full of inside jokes and sarcasm, this one includes some of his beautiful thoughts on the friendship they all shared: "*You have stated very well that there will always be an indissoluble bond which will unite us forever and this bond we hold is Faith, which made us companions on beautiful trips and made it possible for our Society to be founded on solid rock.*"[32]

And then, among all those lighthearted letters from Forte dei Marmi, he does something somewhat supernatural. He looks into the future and invites all of us, in a sense, into friendship with him. Recognizing that Faith is what connects us all in a sacred and powerful bond, he writes in hope that this bond "*with the Grace of God, will bind all the Tipi Loschi in this life and in the next . . . and will*

[30] Frassati, *Letters*, 168.
[31] Frassati, *Letters*, 170.
[32] Frassati, *Letters*, 164.

be the connection through prayer to spiritually bond all the Tipi Loschi scattered all over the earth."[33]

Sitting in front of his books for hours on end, Pier Giorgio wrote that every now and then he would *"look out the window and contemplate the sea which is magnificent."*[34] It was in the vastness of that view that he envisioned friendships forged in faith lasting forever. Somewhere off in the horizon, there we (the modern-day Tipi Loschi) were.

All I bought at the Forte dei Marmi market was a belt. At the time, I was disappointed. But now, when I wear it, I have a physical reminder of how I am encircled by Blessed Pier Giorgio's love and friendship—what he would laughingly call a "terroristic embrace." What a priceless gift from the sea!

Pray

PRAYER FOR THE FOURTEENTH STATION OF THE VIA LUCIS WITH PIER GIORGIO

O Father, it was Your desire to unite all of Your people
on earth. In the same way, it was the desire of Pier
Giorgio that all of his friends would be bound together
by faith and spiritually connected in prayer. Pour
out Your abundant blessings on all those who share a
love for Your faithful servant Pier Giorgio Frassati.

Blessed Pier Giorgio, pray for us. Amen.

Act

Take time to write a letter of encouragement to a friend today.

[33] Frassati, *Letters*, 167.
[34] Frassati, *Letters*, 163.

10

Living Lent (and Life) Like Blessed Pier Giorgio

In this Holy Lent, let us lift up our hearts and always go forward for the triumph of the reign of Christ in Society.[35]

Several years ago, two of my little nieces taught me a simple Lenten song (sung to the tune of "Frère Jacques") that has since become a favorite of the adults in my morning prayer group:

> Prayer and fasting
> And almsgiving;
> We are meant to repent.
> Forty days of sacrifice,
> Being super extra nice:
> This is Lent. This is Lent.

In a way, these lyrics sum up just about everything I've read describing Blessed Pier Giorgio's Lenten practices. Actually, they sum up how he lived nearly every day of his life. The difference during those forty days may have just been the extra intensity with which he committed himself to prayer, fasting, almsgiving, and sacrifice. (I think he was always super extra nice.)

[35] Frassati, *Letters*, 214.

Finding Frassati

An interesting observation by one of the Frassati housemaids familiar with many of Pier Giorgio's habits was that he was "always carrying around breadcrumbs for his goldfish in Pollone."[36] It is well known that the family had many pets, but I never once heard about the goldfish. After learning about them, I couldn't stop thinking about the crumbs that the maid said Pier Giorgio carried.

There is a lesson in those crumbs. The same guy who would carry breadcrumbs around for his fish would haul a poor family's belongings through the streets in a wooden cart; he would give his bus ticket to someone in need and have to run home; he would spend hours on his knees before the Blessed Sacrament; and he would go without food or water even on a mountain climb if it meant keeping the fast before Mass. No, not just during the season of Lent but every single day, Blessed Pier Giorgio showed by his actions that he embraced the two greatest commandments. He loved God with all his heart, mind, and soul; and he loved his neighbor as himself. Therefore, no amount of prayer, fasting, almsgiving, or sacrifice could ever be too much.

And me? It's humbling, even painful, to reflect on how I live those two commandments. The truth is that all too often I have been giving crumbs to God. Crumbs are for fish.

⁂

Pray

O Lord and Master of my life, keep from me the spirit
of indifference and discouragement, lust for power
and idle chatter. Instead, grant to me, Your servant,
the spirit of wholeness of being, humble-mindedness,

---

[36] L. Frassati, *Mio Fratello Pier Giorgio*, 102.

42

patience, and love. O Lord and King, grant me the grace
to be aware of my sins and not to judge my brother;
for You are blessed now and ever and forever. Amen.

—Saint Ephrem

Act

Learn the Lenten song above and teach it to others. Don't
wait for Lent to put it into practice!

11

Pier Giorgio's Easter Wish

When you possess peace every day you will be truly rich.

Just before spending his last Easter on earth, Pier Giorgio wrote a long letter to his best friend, Marco, and ended it with this beautiful wish: *"I send you my best wishes, rather just one, but I believe it to be the only wish that a true friend can make to a dear friend and it is this: the Peace of the Lord be with you always because when you possess peace every day you will be truly rich."*[37]

His way of defining "truly rich" might strike some as odd. After all, the level of wealth that surrounded him would have been significant even by today's standards. Pier Giorgio grew up with maids, cooks, gardeners, a chauffeur, and a variety of other household staff whose purpose was to serve the needs of the family. He came in contact with very influential members of various segments of society, from politics to the arts. He traveled and attended balls and casually visited high-ranking Church officials. He was no stranger to the luxuries his family's social standing made possible.

[37] Frassati, *Letters*, 225.

But none of this worldly wealth brought peace into their family life. The tense, strained relationship of his parents is a common theme of most biographies about Pier Giorgio. One story tells of how he finally had to slam his fist on the table during a meal and say, "Enough!" to end the bickering. Money alone, Pier Giorgio personally experienced, did not bring happiness.

In his Easter letter to Marco, Pier Giorgio made clear what he considered to be the source of true riches: peace — the kind that comes from a relationship with the Prince of Peace. We know of at least fifty times that he wrote about peace. It was a frequent theme in his letters to his friends and a frequent lament that he made when he saw how much it was lacking in various situations. Peace, he said, was *the best of all earthly gifts.*[38] Based on his writings, I believe he would willingly have traded all of the material wealth that his family enjoyed for them to experience true spiritual wealth.

Just a few months after writing about peace to Marco, Pier Giorgio was unexpectedly summoned by the Lord. His death left a tremendous void in his home, but it did bring healing to his parents' marriage in a way that had not seemed possible during his lifetime. Through their shared experience of profound loss, his parents found some degree of that once-elusive peace. At great personal cost, the prayers of their son were answered; they had become "truly rich."

[38] Frassati, *Letters*, 191.

Pray

O Blessed Jesus, give me stillness of soul in You.
Let Your mighty calmness reign in me. Rule
me, O King of Gentleness, King of Peace.

—Saint John of the Cross

Act

Think of how you can be an example of peace at home, at
school, or at work. Greet others today by saying, "Peace be
with you!"

12

Like Father, Like Son

I would willingly have stayed a bit to ski, but I had to reach Berlin because my father is returning to Italy soon and I wanted to spend a few days with him.[39]

❖

One of the pitfalls of learning about people only from books is that it is easy to develop a purely one-dimensional understanding of their characters. I think this is often the case with Pier Giorgio's father, Alfredo.

The impression that people often have after finishing a book is that he was an atheist or an agnostic, that he was a harsh man in an unhappy marriage who had little understanding of his son and even less tolerance for his religious views. This superficial sketch of his character isn't all that unreasonable, given the translation of the few sources available to us in English. But it really isn't an accurate depiction of the man who raised a future saint.

Alfredo Frassati was a high-achieving man from an early age. He did some of his university studies in Germany and was fluent in that language. (This made him an excellent candidate for the position of ambassador to Germany later in his career.)

[39] Frassati, *Letters*, 102.

Finding Frassati

Alfredo loved the mountains and wrote beautiful passages about how being in the mountains made him feel close to God. Sound familiar? He loved the land and had a great interest in agricultural developments. He was a talented sportsman and enjoyed horseback riding with his children. He had a great appreciation for the arts and had high standards for how a man should behave.

He was ambitious. He took a financial risk by borrowing money from his family to purchase the local paper. He was a gifted journalist and editor who assembled a good team around him, and his business venture was a huge success. His *La Stampa* is still a leading Italian daily newspaper.

As both a journalist and a politician, Alfredo held courageous views for the times, even when unpopular and at great personal expense. The infamous rise to power of Benito Mussolini brought Fascism to the forefront. Although holding an important ambassadorship at the time, Mr. Frassati was too great a patriot ever to serve in such an administration, and he walked away from his position. When he resigned, he noted that he would never have been able to face his son had he stayed in that capacity. But his resignation was driven foremost by his interior standards of proper governance and social justice.

Alfredo was not in a happy marriage. Who can know what each spouse contributed to the downfall of the relationship? This definitely created tension in the home and was stressful for Pier Giorgio and his sister Luciana. On the other hand, the home was also a source of much diversion, as it was frequented by many important cultural and political figures.

It was only natural that Mr. Frassati, being so successful in a worldly sense, hoped that his son would follow in his footsteps and pursue a career that brought some degree of fortune and fame. It was hard for him to understand the otherworldliness of Pier Giorgio and why his son would spend so much time in church or in prayer. How could he, as a fallen-away cradle Catholic with little faith, appreciate the fullness of Pier Giorgio's spirituality? But he had great respect for Pier Giorgio and could rarely turn down any request his son made. And he had great respect for the Church. It was very common to have priests and nuns in and out of the home as tutors or caregivers or visitors.

Alfredo Frassati made generous donations to people and places in need. If you visit Pollone, the proof is all around. At his newspaper office, he kept a supply of coal to give to the poor who could not afford it in the winter. His sense of charity, we could say, was primarily of the kind of giving financial resources. It was hard for him to understand a son who removed his shoes or coat and gave them to strangers. But he understood charity. Pier Giorgio learned about caring for one's fellow man from his father and mother, who espoused spiritually conservative values. They went about charity differently, but they all went about it.

Not surprisingly, Alfredo was devastated upon the death of his son. He couldn't bear to hear his name at times or look at a photograph of him. As he slowly made his journey back to the sacraments, he began to understand Pier Giorgio almost better than when he was alive. He missed him his entire life and wrote movingly in his last will and testament about his desire to rejoin him one day.

Pier Giorgio admired his father and was proud of him, but their relationship was complicated. It had to be difficult to grow up in the shadow of such a well-known and influential journalist, businessman, and politician. Although they shared many interests and values, his father's lack of a relationship with the Lord in the Eucharist made Pier Giorgio by default the spiritual head of the household. In their own ways, each wanted more for the other. In their own ways, each left a mark on each other and the world.

Whenever I visit Pollone, I like to stop at the little plaza about a block from the entrance to the family home. There is a monument of Alfredo Frassati there. Important men have monuments.

Finding Frassati

This one sits at the intersection of Frassati and Frassati — the two streets named for Alfredo and Pier Giorgio.

I have to walk a bit farther down Pier Giorgio Frassati Street to reach another monument. It is outside the cemetery and features an image of Pier Giorgio walking with Pope Saint John Paul II. Important men have monuments.

Like father, like son.

Pray

Saint Joseph, guardian of Jesus and chaste husband of Mary, you passed your life in loving fulfillment of duty. You supported the holy family of Nazareth with the work of your hands. Kindly protect all the fathers who trustingly come to you. You know their aspirations, their hardships, their hopes. They look to you because they know you will understand and protect them. You, too, knew trial, labor, and weariness. But amid the worries of material life, your soul was full of deep peace and sang out in true joy through intimacy with God's Son, entrusted to you, and with Mary, His tender Mother. Assure those you protect that they do not labor alone. Teach them to find Jesus near them and to watch over Him faithfully as you have done. Amen.

—Pope Saint John XXIII

Act

If your father is still living, make plans to spend some time with him this weekend. If he is deceased, visit his grave or light a candle for him in church this weekend.

13

The Heart of a Mother

*A Mother's advice is always the wisest and always
the best even when one is already old.*[40]

❦

Adelaide Ametis Frassati loved her son, Pier Giorgio. She had to have been overtaken by the worst kind of fear when he was born with third-degree asphyxiation. It had been only fourteen months since she had buried her baby girl Elda. Would this child also be taken from her before his time? Yes, although not for twenty-four years.

Unfortunately, in the various books about Pier Giorgio, his mother tends to be portrayed as an unsympathetic figure in his life. She was considered severe in her parenting, a cigar-smoking artist whose marriage was on the verge of separation, an emotionally fragile woman lacking the skills needed to run a household.

You need to search closely among the pages to find more positive portrayals of her. For example, during the First World War, she volunteered with the Italian Red Cross to do whatever she could to aid wounded soldiers. It was Adelaide who led Pier Giorgio into the mountains for one of his first climbs of more than ten thousand

[40] Frassati, *Letters*, 87.

feet. She brought the family great honor when one of her exhibited paintings was purchased by the king of Italy.

Pier Giorgio loved his mother dearly. The letters he wrote to her as a small boy reveal the tenderness of their relationship. This continued into his young adulthood. He valued her opinion and sought it often.

When he was twenty years old, he spent some time living with a family in Germany to improve his language skills. He missed his mother when they were separated and openly expressed his love for her. *"You can't imagine with how much joy I read your letter today,"* he wrote, *"and more so because I found in it a photograph of my dear mama, which although is not a great picture is still a remembrance; so I'll have you closer and every night I will be able to see you through it."*[41]

One of the most emotional scenes in the book about the last week of his life is the moment when his mother finally realized the extent of his illness. He cautioned her about getting too close to him, but she quickly reassured him that "mothers never catch their children's illnesses."[42] She didn't catch it, but the next day he was gone. Adelaide lost both her mother and her only son that week. It must have been a crushing level of heartache. But she found the strength to carry on.

After Pier Giorgio's death, Adelaide stopped exhibiting her artwork, although you can still see some of it decorating the walls of the family crypt in Pollone. She helped retrieve letters and photos from Pier Giorgio's friends to preserve the memories of her son that were ultimately so instrumental in advancing his canonization cause. She poured her mother's heart into leaving a legacy

[41] Frassati, *Letters*, 51.

[42] Luciana Frassati, *My Brother Pier Giorgio: His Last Days* (New Hope, KY: New Hope Publications, 2002) 80.

that would endure, that would allow future generations, like ours, to know and love him.

After doing so much on his behalf, Adelaide didn't live to see Pier Giorgio's beatification. Not to worry. She knows about it now.

Pray

MEMORARE

Remember, O most gracious Virgin Mary, that never was it known that anyone who fled to your protection, implored your help, or sought your intercession was left unaided. Inspired by this confidence, I fly unto you, O Virgin of virgins, my mother; to you do I come, before you I stand, sinful and sorrowful. O Mother of the Word Incarnate, despise not my petitions, but in your mercy hear and answer me. Amen.

Act

Pray the Rosary for your mother today.

14

Pier Giorgio's Sisters

*You can imagine my only sister, the companion of
my childhood: to see her leaving for such distant
shores was for me a shot in the heart.*[43]

"Take it away!" Those were the words sixteen-month-old Pier
Giorgio spoke upon seeing his newborn sister Luciana for the first
time. He quickly warmed up to her, and they had a special relationship throughout their lives. In fact, according to Luciana, they
were raised like twins. They started school together and received
the sacraments of Holy Communion and Confirmation together.
It wasn't until Luciana's marriage that they experienced a real
separation from each other.

Largely unknown to many is the fact that Pier Giorgio and
Luciana had an older sister. Elda Frassati was the firstborn child of
Alfredo and Adelaide. She died in infancy, less than nine months
old, in February 1900. The loss of Elda was perhaps one of the
reasons Mrs. Frassati preferred to keep Pier Giorgio and Luciana
together as much as possible. She thought they could protect one

---

[43] Frassati, *Letters*, 203.

another. As she hoped, they became the closest of companions and confided in one another throughout their lives.

The day that newlywed Luciana departed by train for the Netherlands, she saw her strong and secure brother break down with heart-wrenching sobs. He was happy for her but knew how her absence would impact the family and his life in particular. "*Now I will have to fill the void my sister will leave in our home,*"[44] he wrote to a close friend. It was an especially difficult period because their parents' rocky relationship had reached the point of a pending separation.

After his outpouring of emotion when exchanging farewells with Luciana at the train station, Pier Giorgio was determined to press on with the responsibilities of student and family life. But he let her know it wasn't easy.

> *At first living together every day I wasn't able to sufficiently appreciate all that you mean to me, but unfortunately now that many kilometers separate us, now that we must be separated not for a few days but for life and only to see one another from time to time, I understood what it means to have a sister at home and what a void her distance can leave.*[45]

Sadly, less than six months later, it was Luciana's turn to suffer the heartache of separation as she watched Pier Giorgio take his final breath.

Following the death of their mother, it was Luciana who took it upon herself to seek clarification of matters surrounding Pier Giorgio's canonization cause. Eventually, it began moving forward again, and Luciana increased her efforts on Pier Giorgio's behalf. She wrote many wonderful books about him without which we

[44] Frassati, *Letters*, 187.
[45] Frassati, *Letters*, 208.

would have a very difficult time getting to know him. As a result, many of us living outside Italy know her only as the sister and biographer of Pier Giorgio. But she was quite remarkable in many other ways.

In a conversation after Luciana's funeral Mass, one of her sons recounted for me her heroic efforts to free many Polish Jews from sure extermination in Nazi concentration camps. Taking full advantage of her diplomatic passport and her ability to finesse her conversations with the Italian dictator Benito Mussolini, she saved many lives.

In addition, she was an accomplished poet and authored many works. She published in-depth historical books on places such as Genoa and Turin, and she completed an extensive multivolume biographical work of her famous father, Alfredo Frassati.

In her humility, Luciana never put herself in the same category as her brother, Pier Giorgio, who, she would say, like Mary of Bethany, chose the better part. *"I started wearing my first long dresses, I became concerned about feminine things, I started worrying about my hat being one way and my dress another. He, on the other hand, was tirelessly directing his steps on the way of religion."*[46]

One lesson from the wide variation in the lifespans and lives of these three siblings, Elda, Pier Giorgio, and Luciana, is that we should appreciate our family members while they are with us. It is also a challenge to us to make today the day we commit to following a path of holiness. We cannot know whether we will be given 8 months, 24 years, or more than 105 to spend in this life. We can be sure, however, that what we do with whatever time we are given in this life will make all the difference in how we spend the next one.

[46] L. Frassati, *Mio Fratello Pier Giorgio*, 20.

Finding Frassati

Pray

PRAYER TO SEEK GOD CONTINUALLY

O Lord, my God, I believe in You, Father, Son, and Holy Spirit. Insofar as I can, insofar as You have given me the power, I have sought You. I became weary and I labored.

O Lord my God, my sole hope, help me to believe and never to cease seeking You. Grant that I may always and ardently seek out Your countenance. Give me the strength to seek You, for You help me to find You and You have more and more given me the hope of finding You.

Here I am before You with my firmness and my infirmity. Preserve the first and heal the second. Here I am before You with my strength and my ignorance. Where You have opened the door to me, welcome me at the entrance; where You have closed the door to me, open to my cry; enable me to remember You, to understand You, and to love You. Amen.

—Saint Augustine

Act

Let your brothers and sisters know that you love and appreciate them today.

15

The Love of an Italian Grandmother

I will be at home to keep grandmother company for awhile.[47]

I have always enjoyed knowing that Pier Giorgio and I both had a grandmother named Josephine. Mine was extra special because she was the only grandparent I knew. (The other three died before I turned five.) She lived close by and was a constant presence in our lives, not to mention the source of *delizioso* homemade ravioli and bread and other great dishes.

My Italian grandmother was my motivation for trying to learn the Italian language; after one semester, I realized that she spoke a dialect you couldn't learn in a classroom. My brothers and sisters and I still do a fun impersonation of her distinct voice. My last visit to her before she died was to bring her a piece of my birthday cake. She was so animated and told me wonderful stories. I didn't understand a lot of what she said, but I loved being with her. There is nothing like an Italian grandmother!

Pier Giorgio was blessed to have the love of two Italian grand-mothers throughout his life. His paternal grandmother, Josephine

[47] Frassati, *Letters*, 73.

Finding Frassati

Frassati (Giuseppina, in Italian), played a key role in the family's financial situation. She generously gave her life savings to her son Alfredo so that he could take control of the local newspaper, which he renamed *La Stampa*. Alfredo's journalistic success with the paper set him on course for his political career, which, in turn, had a big impact on Pier Giorgio's life experiences. Josephine Frassati outlived her grandson Pier Giorgio by eight years.

Pier Giorgio's maternal grandmother, Linda, was tied more closely to his life in a spiritual sense. She taught him the importance of always remembering the holy souls in Purgatory, a lesson he put into practice often by praying the De Profundis.

Linda's husband, Pier Giorgio's grandfather Francesco Ametis, built the family home in Pollone. It was the location of many happy occasions for Pier Giorgio, picking flowers, helping in the garden, climbing the nearby mountains, tending sheep, and so much more.

On May 25, 1925, a few weeks before Linda's death from natural causes, Pier Giorgio wrote to his best friend, Marco, *"I ask you to pray for my Grandmother, who unfortunately is not at all well, luckily it's nothing serious right now but at 86 years of age her condition can change from one moment to the next."*[48] A second time, on June 5, he wrote again asking for prayers because she was still not well. Naturally, all of the focus in the home was on his grandmother during this period. As Pier Giorgio's own physical condition began unexpectedly to deteriorate, his suffering went largely unnoticed. Death swept in swiftly, taking Linda on July 1 and Pier Giorgio on July 4.

Losing close family members, including both of my parents, has caused me to reflect more on the impact people have on our lives. Too often, we don't even realize it until it is much too late. Pier

[48] Frassati, *Letters*, 234.

Giorgio's life was obviously profoundly and positively impacted by his family members. His character, his happiness, his sorrows, his life, and even his death all were shaped in some way or another by those most intimate relationships.

It is unfortunate that more of a focus is often placed on the severity of Pier Giorgio's parents when he was young, the discord in the home because of their marital difficulties, or their failure to understand his spirituality. We should focus instead on the fact that there was a lot of love in his life. His parents and sister loved him dearly, as did his aunts and uncles, grandfathers, cousins, and many friends.

And he had the love and admiration of not one Italian grandmother but two. I'm only a little envious.

Pray

DE PROFUNDIS (PSALM 130)

Out of the depths I call to you, LORD;
    Lord, hear my cry!
May your ears be attentive
    to my cry for mercy.
If you, Lord, keep account of sins,
    Lord, who can stand?
But with you is forgiveness
    and so you are revered.

I wait for the LORD,
    my soul waits
    and I hope for his word.
My soul looks for the Lord
    more than sentinels for daybreak.

Finding Frassati

More than sentinels for daybreak,
   let Israel hope in the LORD,
For with the LORD is mercy,
   with him is plenteous redemption,
And he will redeem Israel
   from all its sins.

Act

Visit, call, write to, and pray for your grandparents as often as possible.

16

Telegrams, Texts, and Test Scores

*I received your telegram today . . . and with great
pleasure I read about your 90 kisses.*[49]

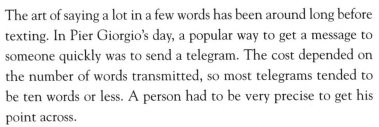

The art of saying a lot in a few words has been around long before
texting. In Pier Giorgio's day, a popular way to get a message to
someone quickly was to send a telegram. The cost depended on
the number of words transmitted, so most telegrams tended to
be ten words or less. A person had to be very precise to get his
point across.

Because of their social standing and the travels required by
Ambassador Frassati's career, many telegrams were sent between the
family members. A particular bit of news that warranted spending
money on a telegram was the grade Pier Giorgio received on any
of his university exams. The progress he was making toward his
degree was definitely of interest to his parents, as his studies were
a regular source of struggle for him.

In November 1922, Pier Giorgio took the exam in construction
science, the last class he had to pass in order to begin year four of

[49] Frassati, *Letters*, 81.

his engineering studies. He victoriously sent the following cryptic telegram to his parents in Berlin on November 6:

Guidi 75 kisses[50]

Although obscure to us, his parents would have understood his code perfectly. Guidi was the professor for the course; "75 kisses" meant that he scored a 75 on the exam. I like to picture Pier Giorgio heading to the telegraph office and dictating that little note to the operator with a great sense of relief. And it must have put a smile on his parents' faces when they were handed the telegram and read those few words. He passed!

Like his father and sister, Pier Giorgio was an exceptionally gifted writer and was able to get his point across, whether in a short telegram or a long letter. Over the years, he wrote many amusing descriptions of mountain climbs and adventures with his friends. He shared profound reflections about life and love and the great gift of faith. He even communicated in more than one language.

Pope Saint John Paul II left instructions in his will to have his own personal notes and letters burned after he died. His secretary could not bring himself to do it and eventually published them. I doubt that it ever crossed Pier Giorgio's mind that complete strangers would be reading his personal letters decades after his death. Thanks to the efforts of his mother and sister, many have been made available.

It may seem like an invasion of privacy to read things someone never intended to share. On the other hand, if you want a window into the soul of a saint, the best place to go is straight to the source. And, in the case of Pier Giorgio's letters, you might just find a few heavenly kisses tucked inside.

[50] Frassati, *Letters*, 99.

Pray

SAINT THOMAS AQUINAS'S PRAYER BEFORE WRITING

O Creator of the universe, Who has set the stars in the
heavens and causes the sun to rise and set, shed the
light of Your wisdom into the darkness of my mind.
Fill my thoughts with the loving knowledge of You,
that I may bring Your light to others. Just as You can
make even babies speak Your truth, instruct my tongue
and guide my pen to convey the wonderful glory of
the Gospel. Make my intellect sharp, my memory
clear, and my words eloquent, so that I may faithfully
interpret the mysteries that You have revealed.

Act

Although quite different from ours, the technology of Pier
Giorgio's day still presented plenty of time-management pitfalls. This didn't stop Pier Giorgio from reaching the heights
of holiness. Try to block out a period of time each day free
from all technology. Silence your phone for the next fifteen
minutes. Delete an app that wastes a lot of your time. Now
that you have some quiet time, plan to read Pier Giorgio's
letters!

17

A Cup of Joe

I should leave off now because I'm going to
bring a cup of coffee to Dr. Engel.[51]

On Tuesday mornings, I have a standing coffee date with a friend. We have a few favorite places and enjoy just sitting, sipping, and chatting about life for an hour or more. Our routine probably wouldn't work very well in Italy.

If you have ever stood at an Italian coffee bar on any given morning, you know that coffee there is nothing like coffee here in the United States. For starters, there's the size difference. Those wee cups of espresso hardly seem worth going to the trouble of interrupting your morning commute for. Forget about parking in some cozy booth with your laptop for hours on end. One or two swallows, and the coffee is gone! And then there's the obvious taste difference. Drinking that small, somewhat bitter espresso is an acquired taste, and one that is often not acquired by Americans who are used to topping off an oversized mug of coffee with half-and-half and their favorite sweetener.

[51] Frassati, *Letters*, 36.

Finding Frassati

That context might help when thinking about Pier Giorgio as a coffee drinker. Although it would have been a tiny cup, he very often had coffee with his friends, and, like many university students, he relied on caffeine to help him prepare for exams. In a letter to his best friend just a few months before his death, he wrote, "*I had to drink huge doses of coffee so that I could study.*"[52]

According to his mother, on days that he fasted at home, he would have black coffee for breakfast. While away in Germany, Pier Giorgio wrote to relieve her concerns about whether he was getting enough to eat. His daily routine included what he described as characteristic German coffee. "*Now, dear mama,*" he wrote, "*I'll tell you what I am eating and how many times. I have breakfast at 7 in the morning; bread, coffee, milk, butter and marmalade. . . . At four in the afternoon coffee the same as at midday. So, you see, dear mama, that I am very well.*"[53]

Often when studying the lives of saints, we can become intimidated or discouraged and think that we can never be like them or be one of them. They manage to deprive themselves of many things with a discipline that seems out of reach for us. For example, on a visit to Ars, I learned that Saint John Vianney existed on a boiled potato or just a piece of hard bread on the days when he even ate anything at all. If that is the daily diet for becoming a saint, I doubt there would be many!

Blessed Frassati had great discipline, of course, and fasting was a regular part of his spiritual practices. But he wasn't a man of unattainable extremes. The ordinariness of his life is one of the reasons his way to holiness is so appealing. He had to deal with many of the same things we deal with in the usual course of a day.

[52] Frassati, *Letters*, 220.
[53] Frassati, *Letters*, 52.

A Cup of Joe

Sure, coffee is such a little thing. But knowing that it was a part of his daily routine makes my Tuesday-morning coffee times even more special. And it's comforting to know that the path to holiness doesn't require a detour around the coffee shop. If only the rest of the journey was as easy as sipping a cup of joe!

⸻⸻❀⸻⸻

Pray

Saint Drogo, patron saint of coffee drinkers, pray for us!

⸻⸻❀⸻⸻

Act

Is there someone you have been meaning to catch up with? Don't put it off any longer. Set up a coffee date.

18

Frassati's Favorite Music

Last night I went to the opera which I enjoyed very much.[54]

Although I have been a symphony-goer for decades, I am still very much a novice in the world of classical music. Pier Giorgio, on the other hand, grew up immersed in culture and had a well-trained ear. His voice was far from well trained, however, as he was tone deaf. By all accounts, his great passion for singing was a source of irritation for those who had to listen to him!

Because Pier Giorgio looks and seems so contemporary, it is easy to forget that he never heard of Bluetooth headphones, smartphones, or digital streaming. In his lifetime, both the radio and the phonograph were fairly new, and, in the absence of television, music videos wouldn't come along for many decades. There was no Internet, no social media, no reality talent shows. But Pier Giorgio knew music. He loved music. According to his sister, he was very moved by music, especially liturgical music.

Most of the music he heard was probably in the setting of a live performance, a school or church choir, a band, a symphony, or

[54] Frassati, *Letters*, 66.

an opera. He loved the works of Giuseppe Verdi but had a broad range of musical interest. For example, in less than one month in 1921, he saw three performances by three composers in three countries. In Germany, he saw *Mignon*, an opera by Ambroise Thomas. In Prague, at the invitation of a priest friend, he enjoyed a well-performed Czech opera, *Two Widows* (*Dve Vdovy*) by Bedřich Smetana. In Vienna, he saw Mozart's two-act masterpiece *Don Giovanni*. Were these the musical preferences of all twenty-year-old Italians at the time?

It isn't clear how often Pier Giorgio went to the opera and the theater, but it was probably quite frequent. His social standing, his family's financial situation, and his various travels would have allowed him to enjoy such opportunities on a regular basis. As the son of a journalist and a well-known politician, he often would have had free entrance to theaters and opera houses and seats on the main floor. But he wasn't pretentious and definitely not above sitting in what we would call the cheap seats. When he went to performances with his friends, which was most often the case, he preferred to sit with them in the uppermost areas of the venues.

Taking time to listen to the music Pier Giorgio listened to has deepened my understanding of how he enjoyed his time on earth. But he made it clear in a letter to his friend Antonio Villani that no opera could ever replace the music he most longed to experience. *"The day that the Lord will choose,"* he wrote, *"we'll find ourselves together again in our true Homeland to sing the praises of God."*[55]

Sing on, Pier Giorgio. Sing on.

---

[55] Frassati, *Letters*, 122.

Pray

I will sing to the LORD all my life;
I will sing praise to my God while I live.
May my meditation be pleasing to him;
I will rejoice in the LORD.

—Psalm 104:33–34

Act

Step into Pier Giorgio's world and listen to a song or two from one of the operas mentioned above.

19

Sailing along with Pier Giorgio

*Almost always during the free time from studying there was
no wind but the other day we went sailing for a long time
and I thought that you would have enjoyed it a lot.*[56]

The quote above is from a letter Pier Giorgio wrote to his aunt
Elena from the seaside town of Forte dei Marmi, where he spent
the first two weeks of the last August of his life. His aunt turned
fifty that year. Because she had always lived with the family, they
had a very close relationship. I have more than forty nieces and
nephews of my own, so the bond between Pier Giorgio and his
aunt is especially meaningful to me.

Pier Giorgio shared his aunt's passion for sailing, and, over the
years, he made a point to send her a note now and then from the
beach. At age fourteen, from Alassio, he wrote: *"I'm so very sorry
that you also were not able to be with us to go swimming. Today . . .
there's a good wind for sailing. I might take a sailboat trip to the island of
Gallinara."*[57] Again from Alassio at age sixteen: *"Two or three days
ago I went sailing in Mascardi's Jole; it was fun speeding along except*

[56] Frassati, *Letters*, 168.
[57] Frassati, *Letters*, 13.

that it took on a lot of water. Who knows how happy you would have been if you had been here![58]

The stereotypical image of Pier Giorgio is one of him climbing the mountains, but, like most Italians, he spent quite a bit of time by the seaside. I can picture him out on the water, enjoying the spectacular coastal scenery in that region. When he got back to shore, he would work on his tan and then give reports on it. *"We are already totally black,"*[59] he wrote to his dad one year. To his mother, *"My back is all peeling because of that ointment and it was already very dark."*[60] Writing from Albisolla Marina to his friend Antonio, *"I've already been swimming a lot and I've already gotten very black."*[61]

What summer activities could be more normal than swimming and sailing and getting a suntan? Yet this is what is so foundational to the spirituality of Blessed Frassati. As Pope Saint John Paul II said to the young people of Rome in 2005, "Get to know him! The life of this 'normal' young man shows that we can be holy by living our friendships, studies, sports and service to the poor in a constant relationship with God."[62]

When I think of the life of Pier Giorgio and how easy it is to relate to him, I'm reminded of a quote attributed to Saint Catherine of Siena: *"All the way to heaven is heaven."* Why do we make holiness harder than it needs to be? After all, God didn't make it impossible for us to find our path back to Him. And it shouldn't be a miserable journey.

This is why I love the example of Pier Giorgio and the freedom his life gives us to live ours. No need to overcomplicate things. We

[58] Frassati, *Letters*, 15.
[59] Frassati, *Letters*, 3.
[60] Frassati, *Letters*, 39.
[61] Frassati, *Letters*, 40.
[62] Address to the youth of Rome in Preparation for World Youth Day, April 5, 2001.

only need to stay in a constant relationship with God, as he did. But this means 24/7 — not just an hour on Sunday. And then we will have the wind at our backs and go sailing along — maybe taking on a little water here and there — until we reach those longed-for heavenly shores. Hopefully, there will be a dark-skinned young Italian saint waving and waiting to catch our line.

———————⟡———————

Pray
Blessed Pier Giorgio,
athlete for God's kingdom,
pray for us!

———————⟡———————

Act
God created nature for us to enjoy. Soak up some sunshine today.

20

Pier Giorgio's Love for Our Lady

*Our Lady is worth a whole lot to the church,
and we owe everything to her.*[63]

A common complaint among many non-Catholics is that the Church honors Mary too much. How much honor could be too much for the Mother of God? For Blessed Pier Giorgio, this devotion was a core component of his spirituality.

He belonged to many Marian organizations and prayed the Little Office of Our Lady. A very tangible witness of his all-consuming love for her was pinned to his study door: his handwritten copy of Saint Bernard's Hymn to the Virgin from Dante's *Paradiso*.

Like many of us, he had a special fondness for her under one particular title: the Madonna of Oropa. (His other favorite was Our Lady of Consolata in Turin.) According to a centuries-old local legend, the Madonna of Oropa is one of the black statues carved by Saint Luke and brought to Oropa by Saint Eusebius. According to a more recent legend, Pier Giorgio ran off to see her every single morning that he spent in Pollone. *This is definitely a legend!* His actual practice was to make a special trip to the shrine to pray at her feet upon arriving in and before departing from Pollone. Fittingly, his portrait now hangs in a side chapel there.

One of the simple joys I experienced whenever I stayed at the family home in Pollone was literally taking time to smell the roses. They grow in abundance in a variety of colors along the garden path. In the summer, a fresh-cut bouquet can always be found in Pier Giorgio's bedroom. If he were alive, he would probably take them right from the vase and bring them to his beloved Madonna of Oropa!

"Flowers were his fervent and most obvious homage to the Blessed Virgin," his sister Luciana wrote. "Wherever there was a celebration in her honor, Pier Giorgio would show up with a bunch of flowers. He did this from the time when he was a student at the Sociale, in other words, from when he was a young boy."[64]

After his death, several people shared testimonies of seeing Pier Giorgio walking to the shrine with flowers from the family garden. The priests there were particularly impressed by his visits in the winter snow. "We were amazed, and would say, 'Why are you here in this weather, Pier Giorgio?' He would answer, '*I've brought some flowers for Our Lady.*'"[65]

Nearly every image we have of Pier Giorgio brings to mind a strong, handsome, athletic figure with a hint of a confident swagger. It's beautiful to picture that same young man, so full of love for Our Lady, humbly cutting and carrying flowers to her.

Of course, the flowers were not the only or even the best gift he brought to her. His rosary was his constant companion, and he favored Our Lady with a daily bouquet of prayers, as well. According to Pier Giorgio's best friend, Marco, "a day never passed that

[64] L. Frassati, *Mio Fratello Pier Giorgio*, 165.
[65] L. Frassati, *Mio Fratello Pier Giorgio*, 172.

he didn't weave at the feet of his heavenly Mother the crown of her favorite prayer."[66]

He was a master weaver, if ever there was one. How beautifully adorned Our Lady must have been on the day they finally met.

Pray

Hail Mary, full of grace,
the Lord is with You.
Blessed are You among women,
and blessed is the fruit of Your womb, Jesus.
Holy Mary, Mother of God,
pray for us sinners now
and at the hour of our death. Amen.

Act

Is there an outdoor statue of the Blessed Mother near you? Bring to the statue a bouquet of flowers for Our Lady and pray a decade of the Rosary there.

[66] L. Frassati, *Mio Fratello Pier Giorgio*, 292.

21

The Little Office of the Blessed Virgin Mary

Know that the great Christian family is praying for you.[67]

I was introduced to the Liturgy of the Hours on my very first morning in Nashville, back in 1995, and I have been praying it ever since—still with several of the people who introduced me to it—only now I've graduated to the large-print edition. Realizing this important prayer was also a component of Blessed Frassati's spiritual life highlights for me the beautiful rhythm and continuity of the Church throughout the ages.

Pier Giorgio faithfully prayed the shorter form called the Little Office of the Blessed Virgin Mary because this was the form required when he became a member of the Dominican Laity at the age of twenty-one. He explained to one of his friends, *"We need to recite the Dominican Office of Our Lady or the Rosary every day, but if you deliberately omit this for one day or for a few days you don't commit a mortal sin."*[68]

Many people do not realize that the Liturgy of the Hours (also referred to as the Divine Office or the Breviary) is the public prayer

[67] Frassati, *Letters*, 114.
[68] Frassati, *Letters*, 138.

of the Church, second only to the Holy Sacrifice of the Mass. It adds rhythm to the day and does indeed connect those who pray it to the great Christian family. In fact, in a sense, Catholics have been praying the Office since the time of Christ, because it is rooted in the Jewish prayer tradition.

Much as in Pier Giorgio's day, the times we are living in call for an increase in prayer. Short on time? The truth is we can always find the time for things that are important to us. Pier Giorgio managed to fit prayer into his busy day no matter where he was or what was on his schedule. Someone saw him one day on the tram immersed in his book and asked, "What are you doing, Pier Giorgio?" He answered with a smile, *"I'm saying my Office."*[69]

A priest in my former parish shared with our Breviary group a humorous pact made by some fellow priests. Should one of them die, the others agreed to find his Breviary and be sure all of the ribbons were in the right place so that no one would think he had grown lax in his prayer life. Priests, you see, have an obligation to pray the Office daily. For laypeople, it is encouraged but not required.

No matter what your vocation, staying committed to daily prayer is an essential part of the holiness formula. It keeps you out of the weeds and on the right path. Pier Giorgio knew this and modeled it for his friends so well that, according to his sister Luciana, they found his prayer book after his death "on his bedside table, open and well-worn."[70]

May our prayer books be likewise found—faithfully used and not covered with the dust of good intentions. And, of course, with all the ribbons in the right place.

[69] L. Frassati, *Mio Fratello Pier Giorgio*, 208.
[70] L. Frassati, *Mio Fratello Pier Giorgio*, 199.

———————— ✦ ————————

Pray

Lord open my lips
and my mouth will proclaim your praise.

—Psalm 51:17

———————— ✦ ————————

Act

There may be a Breviary group at your parish. If not, maybe you could start one with the help of your pastor. If you are not already praying a version of the Divine Office, the Little Office of the Blessed Virgin Mary, which Pier Giorgio prayed, may be a great place to start. There are many online sources of information about the origin of these prayers and how to pray them. At first, it may seem confusing or overwhelming, but it gets easier with practice. Try it!

22

O Come, Let Us Adore Him

The rulers of the night take their turn in guarding their castles.
And we owe greater honor to Jesus than to other rulers.[71]

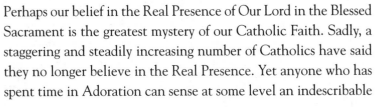

Perhaps our belief in the Real Presence of Our Lord in the Blessed Sacrament is the greatest mystery of our Catholic Faith. Sadly, a staggering and steadily increasing number of Catholics have said they no longer believe in the Real Presence. Yet anyone who has spent time in Adoration can sense at some level an indescribable peace.

For many years, I was committed to the 2:00 to 3:00 a.m. time slot for First Friday Adoration at a local parish. Occasionally, when I was traveling for work and unable to make it, the only person I could find to take my hour was a good friend who happened to be Baptist. Although she did not understand or share my belief in the Real Presence, she felt something so real in the chapel that she was always eager to go back. It wasn't some*thing* she felt, I tried to explain; it was some*one*.

Eucharistic Adoration in the middle of the night was routine for Blessed Pier Giorgio. As a member of the university's student

---

[71] L. Frassati, *Mio Fratello Pier Giorgio*, 145.

Adoration society, he was assigned the second Saturday of the month at the church of Santa Maria di Piazza in Turin. Although he had a reputation for being riotously funny, when he was before the Lord in the Blessed Sacrament, Pier Giorgio's demeanor was quite the opposite. Often, he would never move a muscle. Hot candle wax could drip on him, and he wouldn't notice. Those who saw him were inspired to greater reverence.

On one occasion, Pier Giorgio mistakenly showed up at the church around 9:00 p.m. on a night when Adoration was assigned to the members of the religious congregation who lived there. Standing in the doorway, Brother Lodovico tried every possible way to persuade Pier Giorgio to go home. He insisted on staying until Brother Lodovico finally gave in "just to make him happy."[72]

Pier Giorgio took his place in one of the brothers' choir stalls. As the night wore on, Brother Lodovico noticed what he described as all the holy tricks that Pier Giorgio used to stay awake when he became drowsy. According to the practices at the time, Pier Giorgio was able to request and receive Holy Communion early in the morning. He did that at 4:00 a.m., spent an hour making his thanksgiving until 5:00 a.m., and then headed out in peace just as the church opened to the public.

Out of concern for his health, Pier Giorgio's mother tried to hide the flyers advertising the all-night Adoration times and places that were sent to their home. But nothing could stop him, even at nineteen years old, with an active student life, from getting to Adoration as often as possible. He considered it a privilege to stand guard regularly in this way with the King of Kings.

We live in a world where we are constantly bombarded by noise and commotion. Our Lord in the Blessed Sacrament wants to draw us away from the world and into a silent communion with Him. He

[72] L. Frassati, *Mio Fratello Pier Giorgio*, 155.

invites us, like Pier Giorgio, to spend time in His presence, to be still and hear His voice. Like Pier Giorgio, let us accept the invitation.

Pray

FATIMA PARDON PRAYER

My God, I believe, I adore, I hope, and I love You! I beg pardon for those who do not believe, do not adore, do not hope, and do not love You. Amen.

Act

The first Friday of each month is a traditional time to devote to the beautiful practice of Eucharistic Adoration. But every day is a good day to spend time in the presence of the Lord. Find a church near you with Adoration and spend some time in quiet contemplation. Put it on your schedule and make it a regular part of your spiritual life.

23

The Great Family of Saint Dominic

*I'm very glad that you want to become a member of
the great family of St. Dominic, where, as Dante says,
'You grow fat if you don't rant and rave.'* [73]

Members of the Dominican Order have an expression to reflect
their individuality that goes something like this: When you've met
one Dominican, you've met *one* Dominican." Blessed Pier Giorgio
Frassati met and was influenced by far more than one Dominican.

In Turin, he was well-acquainted with the brother priests Filippo
and Francesco Robotti. Father Filippo spent a lot of time providing
spiritual guidance for the working-class men. Father Francesco was
the superior of the community at the time of Pier Giorgio's inves-
titure as a lay Dominican in April 1921. Pier Giorgio's profession
the following year was done by still another Dominican, Father
Reginaldo Giuliani, in the Chapel of Our Lady of Grace in the
thirteenth-century church of San Domenico.

Pier Giorgio even met the future master general of the order,
Father Martino Stanislao Gillet, at least once. "I had the occasion
to meet Pier Giorgio during the ceremonies for some university

[73] Frassati, *Letters*, 138.

student members of the Dominican Third Order," wrote Father Gillet. "They were all nice young men, but I was especially impressed by one who was particularly interesting. He held his head up straight, and his bright eyes revealed someone who could guide and direct others. He radiated such great kindness that people were drawn to him."[74]

It is well-established that Pier Giorgio enjoyed reading the works of Dominican saints such as Thomas Aquinas and Catherine of Siena. His admiration for the controversial figure Fra Girolamo Savonarola is also widely known. Without hesitation, Pier Giorgio chose that for his religious name when he became a Dominican tertiary.

There is a lesser-known connection between Blessed Pier Giorgio and another Dominican, Saint Peter Martyr, a thirteenth-century saint known also as Saint Peter of Verona. Like Catherine of Siena and Savonarola, Peter was a zealous Dominican who made no apologies for speaking the truth. It cost him his life. He is usually pictured with an axe or sword in his head—the fate he suffered at the hands of a heretical assassin. Before dying, he used his finger to write the first words of the Apostles' Creed in his own blood. Definitely zealous!

The church where Pier Giorgio made his profession was in the priory of Saint Dominic, which was in the province of Saint Peter Martyr. For nearly four hundred years, Saint Peter Martyr shared a feast day with Saint Catherine on April 29; the Dominicans now memorialize him on June 4. Neither of those dates was his original feast day, however. That date was April 6, the day of his brutal death. Because it so often fell during Holy Week or the Easter Octave, it was transferred to a date when it could be celebrated liturgically.

[74] L. Frassati, *Mio Fratello Pier Giorgio*, 202.

April 6 is still a significant date but for a different Dominican. Pier Giorgio Michelangelo Frassati was born on that day in 1901. It was Holy Saturday, close to 7:00 p.m., and the local church bells were ringing joyously for the Easter Vigil. The great family of Saint Dominic would never be the same. It was a cause for celebration then and a cause for celebration now.

Pray

May God the Father, who made us, bless us.
May God the Son send His healing among us.
May God the Holy Spirit move within us and
give us eyes to see with, ears to hear with,
and hands that Your work might be done.
May we walk and preach the word of God to all.
May the angel of peace watch over us and lead us
at last by God's grace to the Kingdom. Amen.

—Saint Dominic

Act

Read about Girolamo Savonarola, the controversial Dominican friar who greatly inspired Blessed Frassati.

24

Pier Giorgio's Favorite Saint

I would like you to try to read St. Paul: he is marvelous and the soul is exalted by this reading and we are prodded to follow the right path and to return to it as soon as we leave it through sin.[75]

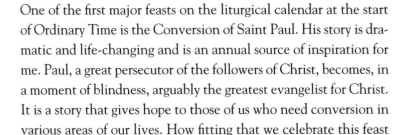

One of the first major feasts on the liturgical calendar at the start of Ordinary Time is the Conversion of Saint Paul. His story is dramatic and life-changing and is an annual source of inspiration for me. Paul, a great persecutor of the followers of Christ, becomes, in a moment of blindness, arguably the greatest evangelist for Christ. It is a story that gives hope to those of us who need conversion in various areas of our lives. How fitting that we celebrate this feast in January, the month for making (and often quickly breaking) resolutions.

I love that the method Christ used to permeate the spiritual darkness in Paul's life was to strike him physically blind. To see fully, in other words, has little to do with our eyesight. When Paul asked the Lord what He wanted him to do, the answer was a simple next step: "Get up and go into Damascus." Paul, being blinded, couldn't possibly find his way alone. So, Scripture tells us, he was

[75] Frassati, *Letters*, 230.

led by hand by his companions (Acts 22:10–11). How gently the Lord worked with Paul and used his friends and even his former enemies to bring him to the understanding of how he would become a great instrument for the kingdom of God.

Blessed Pier Giorgio Frassati did not have a conversion experience like Paul's—not at all. From his childhood, he was disposed to love God, and that love grew until the moment of his death. Yet Saint Paul was his favorite saint and model of charity. Despite their different paths, these holy men had a common denominator underlying their spirituality: the understanding that God is love and that the love of God compels us to love one another.

On January 15, 1925, Pier Giorgio wrote to his best friend, Marco, "*In the world which has distanced itself from God, there is a lack of Peace, but there is also a lack of Charity that is true and perfect Love. Maybe if all of us listened more to St. Paul, human miseries would be slightly diminished.*"[76]

Pier Giorgio so deeply grasped and loved the epistles of Saint Paul that he even gave them in Latin as a gift to a close friend. He also provided the Italian translation because, he said, "*you can better enjoy the beauty of the Latin and better understand the philosophical nexus of the epistles of St. Paul.*"[77]

When he became weary of the engineering material he was required to read for his degree, Pier Giorgio often turned to the epistles as a source of peace, relief, and spiritual enjoyment. Taking time from our busy lives to contemplate the conversion of Saint Paul and immerse ourselves in his epistles can serve a similar purpose for us today.

Reflecting on the life and writings of Saint Paul will sharpen our resolve to perform acts of charity when we feel that virtue growing

---

[76] Frassati, *Letters*, 198.
[77] Frassati, *Letters*, 231.

dull. Further, his conversion story is a powerful reminder that we really can break free from our sinful ways and live for Christ, if only we are willing to seek the true Light that dispels all darkness. *In lumine tuo videbimus lumen.*

✦

Pray

PRAYER FOR THE SECOND STATION
OF THE VIA LUCIS WITH PIER GIORGIO

O Father, you gave Pier Giorgio the clear vision and sure faith to be able to discern the signs of the Resurrection. Remove from our eyes the darkness caused by pride and egoism, and help us to live our earthly lives to the fullest in the light of Your Truth.

✦

Act

Read Saint Paul's recounting of his conversion in Acts 22:3–21.

25

Cultivating a Spirit of Sacrifice

We must be willing to give up our ambitions,
our entire selves, for the cause of the Faith.[78]

As children, one of the expressions my brothers and sisters and I did not like hearing our parents say was "Offer it up!" It was an almost automatic response whenever we complained about something unpleasant we were asked to do or when we didn't get something we wanted. "Offer it up" was a parental discussion-ender. It meant we were not going to get a different answer or outcome, no matter how much we tried.

We didn't understand it then, but what our parents were trying to say was that we should make the sacrifice for Jesus. This act of uniting our sufferings to the Cross allowed us to play a small role in the work of saving souls. Sacrifice, once a central concept in Catholic spirituality, has given way to a desire for instant gratification, pleasure, convenience, and avoiding pain at all costs.

Blessed Pier Giorgio considered a willingness to sacrifice as something absolutely necessary to fight the evil that was confronting his generation. The Church was under attack with regular

[78] Frassati, *Letters*, 130.

persecution by the government. Those trying to remain faithful were enduring hatred and violence. Speaking to a group of young people when he was just twenty-two, Pier Giorgio went so far as to say that without the spirit of sacrifice in abundance, "*you would not be a good Catholic.*"[79]

His view of sacrifice seemed almost radical. It had to be continual, he said. Making a one-time sacrifice was never enough, he said. You have to be willing to give up your ambitions and even your entire selves, he said.

Give up *everything* for the Faith? His idea sounds countercultural even today. Most twenty-two-year-olds might find that level of sacrifice burdensome, if not entirely out of the question. Not Pier Giorgio.

"*Think about what these few years passed in sorrow are,*" he challenged the crowd, "*compared with a happy eternity, where joy will have no measure nor end, and where we will enjoy a peace beyond anything we could imagine.*"[80]

What Pier Giorgio understood so well at such a young age was that life gives us many opportunities to sacrifice, whether we want them or not. Governments will oppress us. Our families are imperfect. The Church has shortcomings. People we love will hurt us. People we depend on will die. But all of these things will eventually pass.

By learning to unite our present sufferings in sacrifice to those of Christ, we can participate in the great work of the salvation of souls. Our reward will be eternal joy.

Mom and Dad were right: offer it up.

[79] Frassati, *Letters*, 130.
[80] Frassati, *Letters*, 130.

Cultivating a Spirit of Sacrifice

Pray

Fatima Sacrifice Prayer

O my Jesus, I offer this for love of You,
for the conversion of sinners,
and in reparation for the sins committed
against the Immaculate Heart of Mary.

Act

Are you dealing with a difficult situation in your life, such as physical pain, financial hardship, loss of or betrayal by a friend, mental anguish, an unpleasant task? Say the above prayer and try to offer up the situation out of love for Jesus.

26

Pier Giorgio's Secret Love

I am reading Italo Mario Angeloni's romance novel
"I Loved That Way" where he describes in the first part
his love for an Andalusian woman and believe me I am
moved because it seems like my own love story.[81]

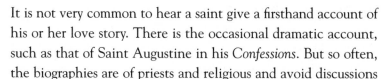

It is not very common to hear a saint give a firsthand account of his or her love story. There is the occasional dramatic account, such as that of Saint Augustine in his *Confessions*. But so often, the biographies are of priests and religious and avoid discussions of affairs of the heart.

In the case of Pier Giorgio Frassati, however, nearly every biography mentions his secret love for a young woman named Laura Hidalgo. And nearly every biography gives a somewhat conflicting account of the relationship. One says he met her while his family was in Berlin. Another says they played together as children, were acquaintances throughout their lives, then struck up a friendship in 1923, after which Pier Giorgio realized he was in love. Yet another says he fell in love in the summer of 1924.

---

[81] Frassati, *Letters*, 190.

Many opinions are also given for the reason the relationship ended, most often placing the blame squarely (but unfairly) on the shoulders of Mrs. Frassati and her supposed outright disapproval of Laura. Some versions of the story say that Laura never knew that Pier Giorgio had feelings for her. Others say she did. One book says within a span of six pages that she both did and didn't know! In one sense, it has become almost as confusing for us to understand Pier Giorgio's feelings for Laura as it was for him when he was struggling with them. Getting the facts right may help.

Laura Hidalgo was not in the same grade as Pier Giorgio. She was three years older and was studying mathematics. Her parents died when she was a teenager, and it fell on her to care for her younger brother. She attended the same Massimo D'Azeglio school as Pier Giorgio, so it is possible their paths did cross on occasion.

In the spring of 1923, during the Italian *carnevale* holidays (similar to our Mardi Gras), Pier Giorgio encountered Laura at Little Saint Bernard, where he would go for good skiing. Laura was a member of the Catholic female university students' club. He was a member of the men's club. There is no question that they developed and maintained a close friendship from that point on because she eventually became a member of his inner circle of friends known as the Tipi Loschi.

It wasn't until the end of 1924 that Pier Giorgio confided his feelings for Laura to Luciana: "He came to me with his great black eyes," she said, "and told me he was in love with a girl I know."[82] This conversation took place more than a year after the occasion when Laura visited the family home for tea—an event that has been frequently mentioned in books and articles. Luciana and her mother had no idea at the time of the tea that Laura had been invited because Pier Giorgio was developing feelings for her. So, it

---

[82] L. Frassati, *A Man of the Beatitudes*, 108.

simply was not true that Mrs. Frassati ever prevented Pier Giorgio from having a relationship with Laura.

What is true is that Mr. and Mrs. Frassati were on the verge of separation, and this was a cause of great concern for Pier Giorgio. He did not want to introduce another issue that would lead to even more discord and family drama. He did not want to begin to build a new relationship on the ruins of his parents' relationship, so he made the painful decision not to reveal his feelings to his parents or to Laura. The choice never to begin dating Laura was completely his to make.

The official canonization documents include the statement that not only had Pier Giorgio said nothing to Laura about his feelings: *he had not even hinted at them.* But he did share his interior struggle over this decision and the grief it caused him in a few letters to his closest friends. It was a very painful period in his personal life. To make matters even worse, at the very time he was relinquishing the idea of a relationship with Laura, his sister was being happily married and beginning her new life.

Reflecting on what he described as his "own love story," Pier Giorgio viewed his decision as cooperation with God's holy will. He made it clear that all he wanted from that point on was the best for Laura. "*I urge you to pray that God gives me the Christian strength to bear it serenely and that He gives her all earthly happiness and the strength to reach the Goal for which we were created.*"[83] Less than seven months after writing those words, Pier Giorgio died and thus reached "the Goal." His prayer for Laura was likewise eventually fulfilled. She married and had children and her share of earthly happiness.

It is easy to forget that the lives of the saints were full of trials, temptations, failures, and struggles—what Pier Giorgio described

[83] Frassati, *Letters*, 190.

as thorns along the path of the purpose for which we are all created. Add heartaches and secret loves to the list.

⚘

Pray

PRAYER FOR THE FOURTH DAY OF THE NOVENA
IN HONOR OF BLESSED PIER GIORGIO FRASSATI

Blessed Pier Giorgio, help me to seek God's righteousness, His plan for my life and for the salvation of the world. Show me the way to self-surrender, so that I may desire nothing more than to be of service to the Lord and His Kingdom. Lead me to the table of love, where I will be satisfied.

⚘

Act

Examine your heart and your loves. Who or what is your greatest love? If it is not God, invite Him again to be the center of your life.

27

Pier Giorgio's Apostolate of Charity

*Every one of you knows that the
foundation of our religion is Charity.*[84]

In the moving account of the death of Pier Giorgio Frassati written by his sister Luciana,[85] his actions in his final hours showed the depth of his compassion for the poor and sick whom he took care of regularly.

It was Friday, July 3, 1925. He would have normally gone that day to the weekly meeting of his Conference of St. Vincent de Paul. Instead, he was bedridden with a fatal diagnosis of polio and surrounded by his grieving family. Almost completely paralyzed at this point, he asked his sister to bring some items from his study and then wrote these barely legible instructions: *These are the injections for Converso. The pawn ticket belongs to Sappa; I had forgotten it, renew it on my account.*[86]

Requests like these would not have come as a surprise to his friend who received this note. After all, this was how Pier Giorgio

[84] Frassati, *Letters*, 239.
[85] L. Frassati, *My Brother Pier Giorgio.*
[86] Frassati, *Letters*, 238.

spent so much of his life—doing one unnoticed act of charity after another. Providing medicine, schoolbooks, bus tickets, food, and clothes; patiently listening; giving time, prayers, love, or whatever was needed was nothing extraordinary for him. He began exercising the virtue of charity as a young boy, and it was a well-defined spiritual muscle by the time he reached early manhood. He became like a member of the family for the people he helped. They knew they could count on him.

Walking the streets of his hometown, Turin, he would have often passed by the inscription *Charitas Christi Urget Nos* (The charity of Christ urges us). Taken from Saint Paul's letter to the Corinthians, this passage is etched above one of the entrances to La Piccola Casa della Divina Provvidenza, known locally as the Cottolengo hospital. It may have been on one of his visits to the sickest of the sick at the Cottolengo that he contracted the disease that took his life. Nobody knows for sure.

Quoting this phrase of Saint Paul in his speech to the youth of Pollone two years before his death, Pier Giorgio added, "*Without this fire, which little by little must destroy our personality so that our heart beats only for the sorrows of others, we would not be Christians, much less Catholics.*"[87] True to those words, his personality was consumed by the charity of Christ.

Not only did he serve the native poor in Turin; his works of charity reached well beyond the Italian border. With his father's appointment to the position of ambassador to Germany, the family began to spend time at the Italian embassy in Berlin. In fact, Pier Giorgio had considered continuing his college studies in Germany during this period. His academic plans changed, but his determination to serve the poor was undeterred wherever he was.

[87] Frassati, *Letters*, 129.

It wasn't long before he made the acquaintance of a German priest, Father Sonnenschein, who was known as the "Saint Francis of Berlin." With Father Sonnenschein's network, Pier Giorgio was back on the front lines of helping the least fortunate, famously giving away even his expensive overcoat to a homeless man on a subfreezing night. This incident confounded his father, who asked him why he had made such an excessive gesture. Because the man was cold was reason enough for Pier Giorgio.

Pier Giorgio also helped the poor in Austria at the request of a friend from the Pax Romana Conference. As always, he preferred to be anonymous. *"There are many children and women workers in Vienna today without a roof over their heads, left prey to hunger and misery,"* he wrote to his friend Maria Fischer. *"I'm sending you 90 thousand crowns that I had left over from my trip and I ask you to use the money as you wish. In this **my name should remain secret**."*[88]

Wherever he went, whenever he saw people in need, the natural reflex of Pier Giorgio was to find some way to help. He saw the light of Christ in each face and was a true apostle of charity, both at home and abroad. Given the extent of his travels, it is impossible to know how many lives he touched. It may be true that charity begins at home. As Pier Giorgio shows us, it certainly doesn't have to end there.

During the homily at the Mass of Beatification, Pope Saint John Paul II reflected on the life and example of Blessed Frassati: "He repeats that it is really worth giving up everything to serve the Lord. He testifies that holiness is possible for everyone and that only the revolution of charity can enkindle the hope of a better future in the hearts of people."

What would a revolution of charity in the spirit of Blessed Frassati look like? What if we all arose each morning determined

---

[88] Frassati, *Letters*, 116 (emphasis in the original).

not to go to sleep until we had done something kind and loving for someone? Imagine a world ablaze with the love of Christ. Not only would such a world be something to see; it would be a wonderful place to live.

Pray

ACT OF CHARITY

O my God, I love You with my whole heart and above all things, because You are infinitely good and perfect; and I love my neighbor as myself for love of You. Grant that I may love You more and more in this life, and in the next for all eternity.

Act

Join "The Pact" by making a commitment to do one small act of charity each day.[89]

---

[89] Learn more at https://www.frassatiusa.org/the-pact-.

28

Pier Giorgio's Apostolate of Persuasion

*How fortunate St. Catherine was
to see Jesus in this life! I envy her.*[90]

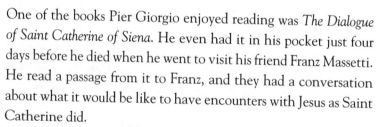

One of the books Pier Giorgio enjoyed reading was *The Dialogue
of Saint Catherine of Siena*. He even had it in his pocket just four
days before he died when he went to visit his friend Franz Massetti.
He read a passage from it to Franz, and they had a conversation
about what it would be like to have encounters with Jesus as Saint
Catherine did.

In this unassuming style, Pier Giorgio modeled for us a powerful and effective way of evangelizing our friends. He called it
the "apostolate of persuasion," and he considered it the most
important and most beautiful apostolate. The way he shared the
spirituality of Saint Catherine with Franz is a classic example of
how he put this apostolate into action. We can break it down
into a few basic steps.

First, he was prepared to evangelize. He was walking around with
a spiritual classic in his pocket. That's what I would definitely call

[90] L. Frassati, *My Brother Pier Giorgio*, 19.

prepared! With technology, we could say we are walking around with a library of spiritual classics digitally accessible, but that's not exactly the same. The book Pier Giorgio was carrying is one that he loved and immersed himself in and was prepared to discuss on a moment's notice.

Second, he wasn't shy about opening the book and reading a page to his friend. That says a lot about the quality of their friendship. Clearly, Pier Giorgio was comfortable talking about spiritual matters with Franz. Are our friends the kind who would welcome a discussion on the life of a saint? They should be. Are we convicted or comfortable enough to share our Faith with our friends? We should be.

Third, Pier Giorgio was enthusiastic about the writings of Saint Catherine. He even told Franz how much he envied her. This not only reveals the extent of his understanding of her words but also gives us a glimpse of the longings of his heart. Meeting the Lord daily in the Eucharist was the center of his life. Meeting Him face-to-face, as Saint Catherine did, was something he yearned to experience. That sort of genuine enthusiasm is what can make the Faith appealing to our friends.

Saint Catherine is noted for saying, "Be who God meant you to be, and you will set the world on fire." I imagine that the conversation with Pier Giorgio that day lit a spark for his friend Franz. I imagine that Pier Giorgio lit quite a few sparks throughout each day of his life. I imagine that he set Turin on fire just being who God meant him to be. In fact, he started quite a spiritual blaze all around the world. Let's keep it burning!

Pray

Precious Blood, ocean of divine mercy: Flow upon us!

Precious Blood, most pure offering: Procure us every grace!

Precious Blood, hope and refuge of sinners: Atone for us!

Precious Blood, delight of holy souls: Draw us! Amen.

— Saint Catherine of Siena

Act

Carry a few holy cards of Blessed Frassati with you — or even a book about him! — and find an opportunity to talk to someone about his life and spirituality.

29

Pier Giorgio's Apostolate of Good Example

The one true joy is that which Faith gives us.[91]

A friend in my morning prayer group is one of those "living saints." Watching how she lives her life, I can understand what Blessed Pier Giorgio meant when he wrote, *"Every day I ought to thank God because he has given me men and lady friends of such goodness who form for me a precious guide for my whole life."*[92]

One morning, as we headed to the chapel, my friend said happily, "This is my best worst Lent ever!" It was the worst because, in addition to several other crosses she had been carrying, she learned that doctors had discovered a tumor, likely malignant, that was going to require surgery. It was the best, she joyfully explained, because the Lord was allowing her to suffer with and for Him even more.

Her ability to welcome another cross without hesitation was hard to comprehend. How we suffer says a lot about us, doesn't it? Her determination to choose joy reminded me of something Pier

[91] Frassati, *Letters*, 190.
[92] Frassati, *Letters*, 224.

Finding Frassati

Giorgio wrote about sadness in the last months of his life that required quite a bit of meditation before I could fully understand:

> *As long as Faith gives me strength I will always be joyful; every Catholic cannot but be joyful: sadness ought to be banished from Catholic souls. Sorrow is not sadness, which is a worse illness than any other. This illness is nearly always caused by atheism. But the purpose for which we have been created shows us the path, even if strewn with many thorns, it is not a sad path. It is joyful even in the face of sorrow.*[93]

For Pier Giorgio, finding a way to keep the joy was an essential ingredient in his pursuit of holiness. It was also a key component of his apostolate of good example. It was important to him to model for others what it meant to be a Catholic young person. One of the secrets to his joy was having his whole life guided by Christian moral law. With that as a foundation, he was able to stand firm in the face of every type of disappointment and suffering that came his way. And they came his way.

Like my saintly prayer-group friend, Pier Giorgio was able to put into practice the formula for joy given by Saint Paul: "Rejoice always. Pray without ceasing. In all circumstances give thanks, for this is the will of God for you in Christ Jesus" (1 Thess. 5:16–18).

Life's circumstances will require us to walk many paths strewn with thorns. During the challenging times, we need to remember, as Pier Giorgio did, that the presence of thorns means that roses are somewhere nearby. When we are able, as he was, to thank God equally for the thorns and the roses, our example can be a powerful witness to the people around us.

It turned out for my friend that her cancer was in stage 1, and no treatment was required beyond the surgery. After having her

[93] Frassati, *Letters*, 210.

best worst Lent ever, she was able to have an extra-blessed Easter season. Through it all, she preached one of the best silent sermons that I have ever heard.

Pray
Thank You, Jesus.

Act
Choose joy today.

30

Politics and Pier Giorgio

I remember the first elections in the time after the war, the
coming of Fascism, and now I also recall with joy that we
haven't been on the Fascist side not even for a single instant of
our lives, but we've always fought against this scourge of Italy.[94]

────────⊛────────

In recent years, it has been nearly impossible to be on the political
fence: you're on one side or the other, and you feel strongly about
it. The same was true in Pier Giorgio's day.

He grew up with politics. His father, Alfredo, become a senator when Pier Giorgio was just twelve years old. Seven years later,
Alfredo was appointed to serve in the prestigious position of ambassador to Germany. Without question, compared with most young
adults then and now, Pier Giorgio was much more informed and
engaged in the day-to-day world of politics.

Watching how politicians behaved made the blood boil in his
veins. (Can you relate?) He loved his country, and he hated what
was happening to it. Writing from the Italian embassy in Berlin to
his good friend Antonio Villani in Turin, Pier Giorgio expressed his
disappointment with strong words: *"I've been so deceived by the really*

[94] Frassati, *Letters*, 155.

shameful behavior of members of the People's Party. Where is the fine program, where is the Faith which motivates our people? Unfortunately when it is a question of climbing after worldly honors men trample upon their own consciences."[95]

According to Luciana, Pier Giorgio could not understand why the Catholic politicians he supported were not behaving in a way consistent with their Faith. He had high hopes for the newly formed party and was disillusioned by what he considered a collapse of the moral responsibility of its leaders. It upset him so much that he wanted to stay in Germany, where he felt as if people still had well-formed consciences and behaved with a sense of responsibility. "*It is peaceful,*" he wrote, "*because it is far from our country fallen into the hands of a band of scoundrels.*"[96]

One difference between Pier Giorgio and most people is that he didn't just complain about what the leaders of the country were doing. He wasn't a sideline-sitter. He tried to make a difference. He knew that charity was not enough, and so he worked to bring about reforms where possible. He participated in gatherings, marched in processions, hung flyers, informed himself on the issues, and worked to persuade others.

There was one other simple action he took to communicate his deeply held beliefs. He would make a large and reverent Sign of the Cross whenever he passed a Catholic church. According to one observer, a public gesture like the Sign of the Cross, at a time when those in politics held strong views against religion, was sure to attract notoriety or, "even worse for a Catholic, [to result in] being called names that were synonymous with 'moron'; that's how fiercely spiritual values were discouraged."[97]

[95] Frassati, *Letters*, 101.
[96] Frassati, *Letters*, 102.
[97] L. Frassati, *Mio Fratello Pier Giorgio*, 113.

Pier Giorgio, of course, didn't make a Sign of the Cross to attract attention of any kind. He did it because he loved God and believed in the Real Presence of Jesus in the tabernacle of the church. And he believed a Catholic man should be a Catholic man inside or outside of politics, whether it was convenient or inconvenient. I sure wish he were running in the next election!

Pray

Blessed Pier Giorgio,
patriotic citizen of the nation,
pray for us!

Act

Is there a group in your area working to defend our right to freedom of religion, particularly the right to exercise our Catholic Faith? Explore ways you can get involved. Pray regularly for our government leaders.

31

"Pumping Iron" with Blessed Pier Giorgio

I beg you to pray for me a little, so that God may give me an
iron will that does not bend and does not fail in His projects.[98]

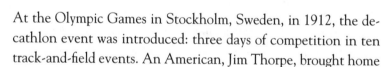

At the Olympic Games in Stockholm, Sweden, in 1912, the decathlon event was introduced: three days of competition in ten track-and-field events. An American, Jim Thorpe, brought home the gold medal.

Back in northern Italy, there was an eleven-year-old decathlete of another kind in training. But there was no medal category for someone who could climb mountains, compete in ski races, bike long distances, swim, sail, canoe, fence, ride horses, pull heavy carts through the streets, and fight off intruders with his fists. If so, Pier Giorgio Frassati would have been a contender!

His athleticism is one of his many relatable characteristics and was frequently mentioned in testimonies collected after his death. The journalist Emilio Zanzi described him as "healthy, strong, and tanned with eyes as clear as pure water."[99] Costantino Guardia Riva, a contemporary of Pier Giorgio who later became an attorney,

---

[98] Frassati, *Letters*, 226.
[99] L. Frassati, *Mio Fratello Pier Giorgio*, 55.

said, "He was so physically strong, he looked exactly the opposite of what one would think an ascetic should look like."[100] How did he get and stay in such amazing physical condition? Basically, he just took full advantage of the opportunities for outdoor activities in every season of the year in the area where he lived.

Although he stayed in great shape, Pier Giorgio was preoccupied with pumping iron of a more spiritual kind. His desire for an iron will is what kept him on the go, whether he was walking the streets of Turin looking for people to help or visiting churches for Adoration. This desire also kept him on his knees.

Pier Giorgio encouraged his friends to work at being stronger spiritually than physically. When his friend Franz decided to get involved in a frivolous activity, Pier Giorgio wrote to admonish him. "And where is Petronius' Iron will? That will which becomes Virtue when it results in self-control. And you who were able to stop smoking when you wanted to, you want to give in to the first temptation."[101]

Pier Giorgio was even more troubled by his own lack of willpower. A few months after he wrote to Franz admonishing him for not having an iron will, he wrote back asking for prayers because he felt he was suffering from the exact same problem. "To put certain plans into action one needs an iron will, which I unfortunately don't have, but instead alas I unfortunately have a will that is used to giving in; so I need prayers because only with them and through them will I be able to obtain from God the Grace to strengthen my will."[102]

Proverbs 27:17 reads, "Iron is sharpened by iron; one person sharpens another." We can make one another better and stronger in the spiritual life by giving good example, admonishing one another

---

[100] L. Frassati, *Mio Fratello Pier Giorgio*, 146.

[101] Frassati, *Letters*, 200. Petronius was a nickname Pier Giorgio assigned to his good friend Franz Massetti as a member of the Tipi Loschi Society.

[102] Frassati, *Letters*, 228.

when we go astray, uplifting one another in prayer. This was why the apostolates of persuasion and good example were so important to Pier Giorgio and why he formed the Tipi Loschi Society for his closest friends.

When someone close to us falls into bad habits or makes unhealthy choices, it isn't easy to speak up and offer fraternal correction. But at least three of the seven spiritual works of mercy challenge us to be the iron-sharpening sort of friend that Proverbs describes. Counseling the doubtful, instructing the ignorant, and admonishing the sinner can be awkward and difficult in any relationship. These weren't easy for Pier Giorgio either. But he cared enough about the souls of his friends to intervene. As he explained to Franz, *"I know that I should not have been preaching because I'm unworthy, but believe that I have been compelled by that Love which unites us, which will be for us a bond of enduring friendship."*[103]

To make progress pumping iron in the gym, a good spotter can be invaluable—not only to help protect the weightlifter from injury but to offer him encouraging words and motivation to reach his desired goals. A good spotter has to be strong and is often stronger than the person lifting the weight. A good spotter has to know when the person is struggling and needs help as well as when to refrain from helping so that the weightlifter can draw on the inner strength to push through the workout.

To make progress in our spiritual lives, a good spotter is priceless. A person who is advancing in virtue can help us avoid sin and persevere on the path of holiness. We should strive to be good spiritual spotters for one another. Help someone pump a little iron will today.

---

[103] Frassati, *Letters*, 200.

Finding Frassati

Pray

PRAYER FOR THE ELEVENTH STATION
OF THE VIA LUCIS WITH PIER GIORGIO

O Father, you inspired Pier Giorgio with the zeal for the apostolate of persuasion. Inspire us with the courage to bring our friends and family members to Christ, especially those who may have fallen away from the Faith. Amen.

Act

Do you have a spiritual director? Ask Blessed Frassati to help you find a holy spiritual director who will be the ideal "spotter" on your journey to the top!

32

Suffering Like a Saint

Who could bear the burden of this life if there weren't
a prize for suffering, an eternal joy[?][104]

During a newspaper interview, I clumsily made the comparison of
Blessed Pier Giorgio with Saint Teresa of Calcutta. "He was like
Mother Teresa before Mother Teresa," I said, "but instead of being
a wrinkled old Indian nun, he was a young handsome Italian guy."
Ouch! Not the best choice of words.

Although far apart in physical appearance, these two great
models of charity do have much in common. Like Mother Teresa,
Pier Giorgio would go into the slums and places where the worst
diseases were present. When a friend asked him how he could
stand the filth and the smell, he said, *"Don't ever forget that even*
though the house is sordid, you are approaching Christ. Around the
sick, the poor, and the unfortunate, I see a particular light, a light that
we do not have."[105]

It was more than twenty years after the death of Pier Giorgio
that Mother Teresa began her mission with the poor on the streets

---

[104] Frassati, *Letters*, 198.
[105] L. Frassati, *A Man of the Beatitudes*, 143.

of Calcutta. She must have seen the same light of Christ around the feeble souls she comforted. How else could she daily walk among such horrible conditions that would repulse most of us? With compassion and tenderness, she ministered to bodies that were nearly dead so that their souls could approach Christ fully alive.

These two humble servants also shared an approach to dealing with suffering. In her writings, Mother Teresa advised, "Never put on a long face. Suffering is a gift from God. It is between you and Jesus alone inside."[106] Only after her death did we learn of the decades-long struggle she had with interior darkness. The joy she radiated from her wrinkled face fooled us into believing she was a stranger to suffering. Rather, she embraced it as a way of sharing in Jesus' thirst for souls. She kept it to herself. It was between her and God.

From his letters, it is clear that Pier Giorgio embraced a similar attitude. Although faced with the departure of his sister from the home, the surrender of his feelings for a girl he loved, the increased tensions between his parents, and the stress of finishing his degree, he wrote, "*I'll always be cheerful on the outside . . . but on the inside when I'm alone I give vent to my sadness.*"[107] His venting was not with anyone and everyone who would listen; it was with Jesus.

Suffering will come into our lives whether we are young or old, strong or weak, saint or sinner. Does striving for holiness mean we are supposed to just grin and bear it no matter how much our hearts may be aching? No. We are called not to be posers and pretenders but to suffer well. Authentic external joy—the joy that put the smiles on the faces of Pier Giorgio and Mother Teresa—follows naturally when we can finally embrace suffering as a gift. Then we

---

[106] Mother Teresa, *A Life for God*, ed. LaVonne Neff (Decatur, GA: Charis Books, 1995), 139.

[107] Frassati, *Letters*, 197.

can also embrace the suffering of others. Then we can see the light around the less fortunate and, with God's grace, run to it.

Pray

DAILY PRAYER OF SAINT TERESA OF CALCUTTA

Dear Jesus, help me to spread Your fragrance everywhere I go. Flood my soul with Your spirit and love. Penetrate and possess my whole being so utterly that all my life may only be a radiance of Yours. Shine through me and be so in me that every soul I come in contact with may feel Your presence in my soul. Let them look up and see no longer me but only Jesus. Stay with me, and then I shall begin to shine as You shine, so to shine as to be a light to others. Amen.

Act

The next time you are at a store or a restaurant, share a friendly smile and a few kind words with the cashier or server. Try to see the light of Christ around the people waiting in line with you. See if this helps to put your own problems into better perspective.

33

Pier Giorgio and "His Poor"

Jesus Christ has promised that all we do for the poor for Love of Him He will consider it as having been done to Himself.[108]

Pier Giorgio's dedication to the poor in his hometown of Turin began when he was a young boy but took on a more systematic nature when he was introduced to the Conference of St. Vincent de Paul.

He was seventeen and back for another one-year stint at the Istituto Sociale, a school run by the Jesuit Fathers — again because of his ongoing troubles with Latin. The first time, at age twelve, the Jesuit Fathers encouraged him to begin receiving Holy Communion daily. Now they would ground him even more in the regular service of the poor with weekly Conference meetings and a steady source of names and addresses of those in need.

Pier Giorgio was so committed to his charitable work that he would often forgo family vacations and remain in the city to care for "his poor." When his sister gave him a share of some money she received as a wedding gift, she told him specifically to use it for himself and not for "his poor." Instead, he split the sum and gave it to two organizations that helped the poor. He even made the donations in his sister's name so as not to get the credit.

On his deathbed, he scribbled a note to be taken to a Conference member with instructions for caring for "his poor." And, at his funeral, it was "his poor" whose presence by the thousands, bewildering to his family, led to the start of his canonization cause. How does a young man reach and touch the lives of so many in just seven short years?

In his service to the poor of Turin, Pier Giorgio would often arrange to meet people "at 6 o'clock beneath the Consolata clock." From there, he would set out on foot to areas of the city that most would be uncomfortable to enter. He kept these holy arrangements faithfully. He was determined in his own "miserable way" to provide material and spiritual comfort to the most desolate. Despite opening his heart and hands to so many, he saw himself merely as "a little twig" who God sometimes used to do good.

And what if that little twig had excelled in Latin? What would have become of "his poor" if he had not been sent to the Jesuit school where he was introduced to the Conferences of St. Vincent de Paul? That academic struggle was such a source of embarrassment for him and his parents, but it became the springboard that took him to much greater spiritual heights. To use the words of the Exultet, it was truly "a happy fault." It is also a good reminder for us that life's disappointments are not always as bad or as permanent as they may at first seem.

Pier Giorgio's impulse to serve the poor reached a crescendo by the time of his early death. His works of charity, largely anonymous, fill an entire book that has not yet been translated into English. The love of Christ urged him, and his love urges us. After all, "his poor" are ours now.

Pier Giorgio and "His Poor"

<hr/>

Pray

Blessed Pier Giorgio, teach me true poverty of spirit. Help me understand that God cares for me and that He asks me, in return, to care for others, especially those in need. Guide me to make choices in my life that will show a preference for service of God and neighbor, rather than accumulating financial wealth and social advantage for myself. Give me a special love for the poor and the sick.

<hr/>

Act

Is there a St. Vincent de Paul organization at your church that takes donations? If not, donate food to a local food bank, clothing to a shelter, or money to an organization that helps the poor. Is there an organization where you can also donate a little of your time?

34

Beggar of Prayers

*Special thanks go to you for the good advice and
for the encouragement that have given me a bit more
strength to face the last storms of my student life.*[109]

Have you ever felt like quitting? Maybe an exercise program, a
novena, a diet plan, music lessons, a sports team, college, a marriage, a job, the Catholic Church, life?

In the Gospel of Luke, Jesus says, "No one who sets a hand to
the plow and looks to what was left behind is fit for the kingdom
of God" (Luke 9:62). But we need grace, a lot of it, to persevere
in life along the narrow path.

So many times, Pier Giorgio wrote to his friends begging for
their prayers. It's beautiful, really, to see that he recognized the
value of prayer, relied on it, and was never afraid to ask for it. Oh,
he had plenty of excuses to be a quitter. His parents did not have
a good marriage, and that made family life stressful. He was called
a blockhead and told that he would never amount to as much
as his sister. He didn't have a very strong spiritual upbringing in

[109] Frassati, *Letters*, 229.

the home, and the time he spent nourishing his soul in Eucharistic Adoration, attending Mass, or serving the poor was often misunderstood.

But he was not a quitter. At age twenty-four, he was still at the university, trying to finish his degree. Ready to move forward with his life beyond academics, he determined that he would study "from morning until evening" to complete his exams and the required thesis. Aware of his own shortcomings, however, and the things that would prevent him from attaining his goal, he turned to the two sources that he knew would sustain him. "*I'm trusting in the Providence of God,*" he wrote to his friend Isidoro Bonini, "*and also in the prayers of friends.*"[110]

God had other plans for how things would turn out for Pier Giorgio; he died before completing his longed-for degree. Similarly, we cannot predict how our own undertakings will end. Regardless of the future outcome, our challenge is to be faithful in living out the will of God for our lives as it manifests itself today.

We do that by persevering in the vocations God has given us. We do that by being the best we can be—the best children, parents, spouses, students, athletes, weightwatchers, musicians, employees, Catholics, patriots, and so on. We do that by not quitting. We do that by setting our hands to the plow and not looking back. We do that by relying on the providence of God and the prayers of our earthly and heavenly friends.

---

[110] Frassati, *Letters*, 226.

Pray

CLOSING PRAYER OF THE CHAPLET OF DIVINE MERCY

Eternal God, in Whom mercy is endless
and the treasury of compassion inexhaustible,
look kindly upon us and increase Your mercy in us,
that in difficult moments we might not
despair nor become despondent,
but with great confidence submit ourselves
to Your holy will, which is
Love and Mercy itself.

Act

Reach out to someone you know is struggling. Let that person know you are supporting him or her with your prayers. If you need prayers from your friends, don't hesitate to ask.

35

Friend of the Friendless

In this earthly life after the affection for parents and sisters,
one of the most beautiful affections is that of friendship.[111]

———————⟨❀⟩———————

When Pier Giorgio decided to start a group of his closest friends, he made sure they wouldn't take themselves too seriously. Their motto set the tone: "Few but good like macaroni." He called them the Tipi Loschi Society, which was a joke in itself. The Italian doesn't translate too well into English, but it means something like "the Shady Ones."

Children often form neighborhood clubs and have special rules and meeting places. Pier Giorgio was twenty-three when he created this group. On the surface, it was very amusing; but it wasn't intended to be all fun and games. His friends were at that point in life where separation was inevitable: new jobs, marriages, and families would mean less time for those mountain excursions they often enjoyed in each other's company, playing and praying together. What Pier Giorgio ultimately hoped the Tipi Loschi Society would accomplish was a lifelong union in prayer, an indissoluble bond of friendship of the most valuable kind.

[111] Frassati, *Letters*, 224.

Finding Frassati

After Pier Giorgio's sudden death, Clementina Luoto wrote a letter to Marco Beltramo that is one of the most moving of eulogies a friend could write for a friend. "Who will wipe away his smile from our memory," she asked, "and who will ever smile at us like that again?" She could only share the depth of her sorrow with the other Tipi Loschi because, as she wrote, "only Laura, Tina, you and Severi know what we six were and what that community of spirit and joy was like that he created. He led and we followed."[112] His goodness united them.

In the Litany of Blessed Frassati, he is described as "Friend of the Friendless." And in an age when people are isolated and finding so little to live for and are turning to suicide in alarming numbers, this particular title is an especially meaningful one. Nobody need ever feel completely alone because everybody can find a friend in Pier Giorgio. You, dear reader, have a true friend in Pier Giorgio.

I realize, of course, that having a heavenly friend doesn't solve all of the problems of someone who feels alone on this earth. But his friendship can be the start of feeling less alone. Ever since I made a connection with Blessed Frassati, he has led me to make connections with others, sometimes in marvelous and almost miraculous ways. I like to think of him as the patron saint of friendship. I really believe he desires to lead us to godly relationships like the ones he enjoyed.

This is one of the reasons it pleases me to see so many organizations springing up under the patronage of Blessed Frassati. My introduction to him came about in this way. When my associate pastor asked me to help start a group for young adults, I could not have imagined that many of those friendships would be so special to me decades later. Good macaroni, Pier Giorgio would say. The best, actually.

[112] L. Frassati, *Man of the Beatitudes*, 166–167.

Friend of the Friendless

Pray

Blessed Frassati, friend of the friendless, pray for us!

Act

Social media simply cannot replace real relationships. If you are in need of a few good friends, why not start praying the Litany of Blessed Pier Giorgio just for this intention? If you're in a good group, look around for people who seem to be in need of friendship, and invite them to join. Let's try to make the world a little less lonely for the people around us.

36

To Lay Down One's Life

What wealth it is to be in good health, as we are! But we have the duty of putting our health at the service of those who do not have it. To act otherwise would be to betray that gift of God. [113]

Betrayal. That word is usually associated with Judas in the garden of Gethsemane or Peter in the courtyard of the high priest. So, I couldn't help but take notice when Pier Giorgio used it in relation to what we do with our good health. It is a strong word choice that reflects his equally strong conviction about our duty to serve the weakest among us.

By all accounts, Pier Giorgio was well built, healthy, and strong. He often enlisted friends who were his physical peers to help him with more difficult tasks. Pulling heavy carts along dirty streets into sordid places wasn't the most appealing way to spend their free time. When his friends let him know how uncomfortable they were going with him on these missions, he reminded them that there, among the sick and the poor, was where the light of Christ shone most brightly. *"You are approaching Christ,"* he told them. [114]

---

[113] From a letter to Willibald Leitgebel, 1923.
[114] L. Frassati, *A Man of the Beatitudes*, 143.

And so it was without hesitation that he set out on each of his visits. He was no Judas.

For years, Pier Giorgio poured out his life in service of the poor and the sick out of love for God and in gratitude for the gift of his own good health. When he contracted the virus (poliomyelitis) that took his life, everyone naturally assumed that it had to have been from an encounter in some slumlike area of Turin. He was known for fearlessly visiting hospitals and people with contagious diseases. Because the virus ravaged his athletic body so swiftly, it was considered a small miracle that none of his family members contracted it.

The consequence of Pier Giorgio's radical love for the poor is a stark reminder that sometimes serving the physical and spiritual needs of others is not convenient and is even risky. It can cost you dearly. It cost Pier Giorgio his life.

To be sure, this element of Pier Giorgio's spirituality is quite heroic and challenging and requires much discernment. After all, as Jesus said, to lay down our lives for others shows the greatest love. That degree of selflessness may not be within our capacity and it may not be what God requires of us.

The duty of putting our health at the service of others will call each of us in a different way. Let us pray, through the intercession of Pier Giorgio, for the grace to respond generously whenever and however it does.

--------- ❖ ---------

Pray

PRAYER OF SAINT IGNATIUS OF LOYOLA

Eternal Word, only begotten Son of God,
Teach me true generosity.
Teach me to serve You as You deserve:

To Lay Down One's Life

To give without counting the cost,
To fight heedless of wounds,
To labor without seeking rest,
To sacrifice myself without thought of any reward
Save the knowledge that I have done Your will.
Amen.

Act

Are you blessed with the gift of good health? Serving others does not always demand that we put our lives at risk. Sometimes it demands that we just get up off the couch to run an errand for someone. Be on the lookout for opportunities to help those who are physically challenged. Drive someone to get groceries or cut the grass for an infirm person or babysit for new parents or ...

37

Pier Giorgio, Public Protests, and Processions

*We should steel ourselves to be ready to carry on the
battles we shall certainly have to fight in order to fulfill our
program and thus to give to our country, in a not-too-distant
future, happier days and a morally healthy society.*[115]

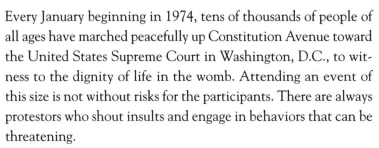

Every January beginning in 1974, tens of thousands of people of
all ages have marched peacefully up Constitution Avenue toward
the United States Supreme Court in Washington, D.C., to witness to the dignity of life in the womb. Attending an event of
this size is not without risks for the participants. There are always
protestors who shout insults and engage in behaviors that can be
threatening.

Taking to the streets to be a witness for his Faith was a regular
activity of Pier Giorgio Frassati. According to Luciana, Pier Giorgio's presence at public processions was an act of courage, not just
a demonstration of his religious principles. Subversive groups tried
to disrupt events "using every means available: hissing, and shout-
ing insults and threats. Pier Giorgio was often assigned the task of

[115] Frassati, *Letters*, 98.

keeping public order.... And so he ran the risk of being punched or, even worse, being arrested."[116]

Although he was arrested on more than one occasion, his style was known to be one of ease and composure when confronted by bullies. He preferred to stay calm in the midst of chaotic situations. Because he was able to deal so well with people, he was placed at the front between the public and the procession to maintain order. He did so by displaying a joyful but firm demeanor, with his rosary in hand and often singing loudly.

Many accounts were recorded by eyewitnesses of the good example Pier Giorgio set during public demonstrations. On one occasion, some women shouted, "They threw a bomb," and pandemonium broke out. Instead of running away, Pier Giorgio hurled himself into the crowd to try to bring it under control.[117]

Just a few days before he died, he was in attendance for a Marian procession in Turin. He was in the front of a bold group of Catholic university students and described as having "his head held high, behaving very reverently and devoutly, and without hesitation." Pushing and shoving was common in these big crowds, and tempers would soon flare. "There was only one part of the sacred procession where such things would never occur," shared an onlooker. "That would be the part controlled by Pier Giorgio, who with his tact and good manners made sure that people thought twice about disturbing the good order."[118]

Publicly standing up to defend religious freedom and the sanctity of life may be uncomfortable for some. May the courageous witness of Pier Giorgio inspire many to holy boldness and help instill an

---

[116] L. Frassati, *Mio Fratello Pier Giorgio*, 122.

[117] L. Frassati, *Mio Fratello Pier Giorgio*, 123.

[118] L. Frassati, *Mio Fratello Pier Giorgio*, 129–130.

unwavering determination to build a morally healthy society and a better future for all.

Pray

Prayer for the eighth day of the novena
in honor of Blessed Pier Giorgio Frassati

Blessed Pier Giorgio, teach me silence in the face of personal humiliation and unjust criticism. But guide me to be courageous like you in standing on the side of God's truth. Help me to be faithful to Him in all things, so that His will may be done in and through my life. Show me how to persevere in the struggle for those things that are holy and honorable.

Act

The next time you are out for a meal in a public place, take time to make a reverent Sign of the Cross and pray before eating. You may be surprised how this simple witness of your faith will impact others around you.

38

Knowing Your Limitations

*I'm just about to leave for a great mountain excursion and
you can imagine the joy that fills my soul right now.*[119]

One of the reasons people often give for their devotion to Blessed
Frassati is his relatability. We find him approachable and can connect with him on many levels. We think that if he can do it, we
can do it. Because he is so normal, he makes the idea of holiness
seem easy or at least possible. Even though we know there will be
obstacles along the way, we forget about them and are drawn along
with him on our spiritual climb to the heights.

He had the same inspiring effect on me when it came to the
idea of tackling physical mountains. I never climbed one before I
got to know Pier Giorgio. Now, for some reason, I have a strong
urge to go to the top when I get near one. Of course, Pier Giorgio
was an incredible physical specimen tackling seriously challenging
peaks. After one of my adventures, my knees and ankles reminded
me for days that relatability with him goes only so far.

[119] Frassati, *Letters*, 181.

Finding Frassati

Nursing my aches and pains, I found it comforting to know that even Pier Giorgio had common sports injuries from time to time. All of his skiing, biking, swimming, climbing, horseback riding, and canoeing and his many other physical pursuits weren't done without an occasional setback.

Just before he turned twenty-four, he injured his left knee in a ski competition. He described it as *"nothing serious just a pinched nerve in the area of the goose's foot."*[120] But more than a week later, it was still an issue for him. Writing to Marco about his plans for Easter he said, *"Everything depends on my leg, if the left knee continues to do poorly, then mediocre plans."*[121] He already had to miss a thirteen-thousand-foot climb of Breithorn with his friends. *"I've accompanied them there in my thoughts,"* he wrote, *"as it wasn't prudent to climb such a height with my knee."*[122]

This is just one more very practical lesson that Pier Giorgio gives us: know your physical limitations. There's a time for climbing and a time for resting. And a little prudence will go a long way in overcoming both physical setbacks and spiritual trials.

Pray

Because you are the smile of God, the
reflection of the light of Christ, the
dwelling place of the Holy Spirit,

Because you chose Bernadette in her lowliness,

Because you are the morning star, the gate of heaven
and the first creature to experience the resurrection,

---

[120] Frassati, *Letters*, 216.
[121] Frassati, *Letters*, 220.
[122] Frassati, *Letters*, 218.

Our Lady of Lourdes, with our brothers and sisters whose hearts and bodies are in pain, we pray to you!

—Pope Benedict XVI

Act

When you get home from Mass, make this Sunday a real day of rest.

39

Passing Time in Pollone

Decide to come and spend a few days here in Pollone.[123]

Each time I am able to return to Pollone is a special time. Driving up Via Pier Giorgio Frassati and arriving at the front gates of the family summer home seems to trigger an inexplicable joy. My soul feels at home and perfectly at peace. It has sometimes rained for days on end during my visits. Most of the time, it is a gentle rain that adds to the peaceful setting. I much more enjoy the sunny days, though, when the mountains are in sight from just about anywhere.

My first trip back after the death of Luciana Frassati was bittersweet. Her spirit had filled the house during all of my previous visits. I loved sitting beside her on the veranda and hearing her voice as she came down the main staircase before meals. A few days before her death, I prayed the Our Father with her in her room. I sorely miss her presence.

Another unseen presence in the house, of course, is the spirit of Pier Giorgio. When I am there, I feel as if he is walking with me in a very real way. I never take for granted that he spent so

[123] Frassati, *Letters*, 89.

much time there. I love to pray in his rooms, but I also enjoy just walking around inside and outside, knowing that everywhere I go he has been.

The flower gardens are magnificent. Pier Giorgio would write about them occasionally in his letters. The view of the mountains from his bedroom window is spectacular. No wonder he struggled so much to focus on his studies while the mountains were beckoning.

Pollone is a very small place; I guess we would call it a village. It takes no time at all to walk to the parish church or to the cemetery. The bells from three small churches mark the time throughout the day. Listening to them makes me think even more about Heaven and what it must be like.

This is surely a bit of bad theology, but I hope Purgatory is like being in Pollone and looking up at the mountains. That is, you feel so close to Heaven that you can almost taste it, and you ache to be on the higher ground. You know there is a greater joy beyond your reach and are unable to cross the void. I know that some saints have given more terrifying descriptions of Purgatory, but I hope it will be like this.

I have occasionally had the pleasure of attending Mass in nearby Oropa at the church Pier Giorgio loved so much and of praying at the feet of his beloved Brown Madonna. One of the most sharply curved roads I have ever traveled takes you to Oropa by car. Unlike Pier Giorgio, I've walked there only a handful of times.

More often, I have had the blessing of attending Mass in the bedroom with the furnishings from the room where Pier Giorgio died. Whether it is in Polish, English, Italian, French, or German, Mass celebrated there is always a moving experience.

What I'm trying to say is, take out your bucket list and pencil this in: "Pass some time in Pollone." You'll be glad you did.

Pray

My holy angel guardian, ask the Lord to bless the journey that I undertake, that it may profit the health of my soul and body; that I may reach its end, and that, returning safe and sound, I may find my family in good health. Do thou guard, guide, and preserve us. Amen.

Act

Until you can get there in person, take a virtual tour of Pollone on the FrassatiUSA website.

40

Come and Pray

*I would like for us to pledge a pact that knows no earthly
boundaries or temporal limits: union in prayer.*[124]

All my life, I've loved the beach. I love the sound of the waves and
the power that emanates from them, the roar and the undulation.
I love the breeze, the sun, the sand, the song of the birds. I love
the beach.

In 2006, I learned to love the mountains. I love the sound of
silence found at the top of a mountain peak and the crisp, cool air
you can breathe there. I love the view of the horizon, the glacier
tops, the clanking of the cowbells from the herds grazing below. I
love the exhausted euphoric feeling upon reaching the top. I never
thought I would, but, thanks to Pier Giorgio, I love the mountains.

What I experience so intensely both at the beach and in the
mountains is God's presence: His greatness, my smallness. My
earthly cares drift out to sea with each wave and into the sky with
each step taken upward along a rocky path. God's assertion of His
majesty to Job comes to mind:

---

[124] Frassati, *Letters*, 197.

Finding Frassati

Where were you when I founded the earth?
Tell me, if you have understanding.
Who determined its size? Surely you know?
Who stretched out the measuring line for it?
Into what were its pedestals sunk,
and who laid its cornerstone,
While the morning stars sang together
and all the sons of God shouted for joy?
Who shut within doors the sea,
when it burst forth from the womb,
When I made the clouds its garment
and thick darkness its swaddling bands?
When I set limits for it
and fastened the bar of its door,
And said: Thus far shall you come but no farther,
and here shall your proud waves stop?
Have you ever in your lifetime commanded the morning
and shown the dawn its place? (Job 38:4–12)

That's quite a bit of boasting on God's part! Perhaps it is His way to remind us that not one of our troubles is too big for Him to handle. Maybe too big for us to handle but definitely not for Him.

Twice a year, the worldwide family of those devoted to Blessed Frassati joins together to pray the novena in his honor. It is such a powerful prayer. Over the years, I have seen much fruit come from it and marvel at the graces received. I have no doubt that Pier Giorgio unites with us and intercedes for us in a special way during those nine days. Still, not all prayers are answered in the ways we hope.

Our job description as pilgrims on this earth is a simple one: to be faithful in prayer, to accept our smallness, and to leave everything in God's majestic hands. He knows best, and not one person is outside of His loving embrace and endless mercy. The graces that await us are more numerous than the sand on the seashore. The peace to be bestowed is more penetrating than the mountain sun. Together with Blessed Pier Giorgio, let us persevere and pray.

Pray

I will extol you, my God and king;
I will bless your name forever and ever.
Every day I will bless you;
I will praise your name forever and ever.
Great is the LORD and worthy of much praise,
whose grandeur is beyond understanding.

—Psalm 145:1–3

Act

Plan to join the next international novena in honor of Blessed Frassati before his birthday or feast day. Or don't wait: start today!

A Closing Note

One of the things about Pier Giorgio Frassati that shouldn't surprise me but always does is how many people identify with him. I have given presentations about his life in the United States, Canada, Italy, and Austria, to people ranging from kindergarten age to ninety-something. The reaction is the same wherever I go.

A chubby middle-school boy in South Carolina, upon seeing a large poster of Pier Giorgio, said enthusiastically, "He could be me!" A thirty-something African woman shared that looking at the image of him on a holy card was the first time she ever connected with a saint. "His life could have been mine," she said. A young Italian woman was so impressed by how much he accomplished in his short life. "He did everything, and he did everything well," she said, "so maybe I can too." Many priests and religious have attributed their vocations to him.

What is it that makes Pier Giorgio Frassati so relatable to people of all ages, from all walks of life, all over the world? The simple answer was given by Pope Saint John Paul II during the Beatification Mass:

> Certainly, at a superficial glance, Frassati's lifestyle, that of a modern young man who was full of life, does not present anything out of the ordinary. This, however, is the originality of his virtue, which invites us to reflect upon it and impels us to imitate it.... He testifies that holiness is possible for everyone.

Finding Frassati

That is really the point of the simple reflections in this book. Being holy does not require extraordinary virtue that is reserved for certain people. We are all called to holiness. The life of Blessed Frassati shows us that it really is possible when we stay in a constant relationship with God—at the beach, in the mountains, in the classroom, at home, with friends, playing sports, drinking coffee, going about our normal, ordinary lives. He did it. You can too.

May Blessed Frassati intercede for you always.

Prayer for the Canonization of Blessed Pier Giorgio Frassati

O merciful God,
Who through the perils of the world,
deigned to preserve by Your grace
Your servant Pier Giorgio Frassati,
pure of heart and ardent of charity,
listen, we ask You, to our prayers and,
if it is in Your designs
that he be glorified by the Church,
show us Your will,
granting us the graces we ask of You,
through his intercession,
by the merits of Jesus Christ, Our Lord. Amen.

Imprimatur, 1932
+Maurilio, Archbishop of Turin

Litany in Honor of Blessed Frassati
(for private devotion)

Lord, have mercy. *Lord, have mercy.*
Christ, have mercy. *Christ, have mercy.*
Lord, have mercy. *Lord, have mercy.*

God our Father in Heaven, *have mercy on us.*
God the Son, Redeemer of the world, *have mercy on us.*
God the Holy Spirit, *have mercy on us.*
Holy Trinity, One God, *have mercy on us.*

Holy Mary, *pray for us.*
All the angels and saints, *pray for us.*

Blessed Pier Giorgio, *pray for us.*
Loving son and brother, *pray for us.*
Support of family life, *pray for us.*
Friend of the friendless, *pray for us.*
Most Christian of companions, *pray for us.*
Leader of youth, *pray for us.*
Helper of those in need, *pray for us.*
Teacher of charity, *pray for us.*
Patron of the poor, *pray for us.*
Comfort of the sick, *pray for us.*

Finding Frassati

Athlete for God's kingdom, *pray for us.*
Conqueror of life's mountains, *pray for us.*
Defender of truth and virtue, *pray for us.*
Opponent of every injustice, *pray for us.*
Patriotic citizen of the nation, *pray for us.*
Loyal son of the Church, *pray for us.*
Devoted child of the Madonna, *pray for us.*
Ardent adorer of the Eucharist, *pray for us.*
Fervent student of the Scriptures, *pray for us.*
Dedicated follower of Saint Dominic, *pray for us.*
Apostle of prayer and fasting, *pray for us.*
Guide to a deep love for Jesus, *pray for us.*
Diligent in work and study, *pray for us.*
Joyful in all of life's circumstances, *pray for us.*
Strong in safeguarding chastity, *pray for us.*
Silent in pain and suffering, *pray for us.*
Faithful to the promises of Baptism, *pray for us.*
Model of humility, *pray for us.*
Example of detachment, *pray for us.*
Mirror of obedience, *pray for us.*
Man of the Beatitudes, *pray for us.*

Lamb of God, You take away the sins of the world,
have mercy on us.
Lamb of God, You take away the sins of the world,
have mercy on us.
Lamb of God, You take away the sins of the world,
have mercy on us.

Pray for us, Blessed Pier Giorgio Frassati,
that we may be made worthy of the promises of Christ.

Litany in Honor of Blessed Frassati

Let us pray: Father, You gave to the young Pier Giorgio Frassati the joy of meeting Christ and of living his faith in service of the poor and the sick. Through his intercession, may we, too, walk the path of the Beatitudes and follow the example of his generosity, spreading the spirit of the gospel in society. We ask this through Christ our Lord. Amen.

Imprimatur, November 2, 1994
+Joseph A. Galante, D.D., J.C.D.,
Bishop of Beaumont, Texas

Resources to Learn More

For much more information about Blessed Frassati, links to various social media and the Casa Maria Bookstore, visit:

www.FrassatiUSA.org

To immerse yourself in Pier Giorgio's writings, read
Pier Giorgio Frassati: Letters to His Friends and Family
(St. Paul's/Alba House, 2009)

For a detailed biography written by his beloved sister, read
A Man of the Beatitudes: Pier Giorgio Frassati, by Luciana Frassati
(Ignatius Press, 2001)

For a moving account of the last week of his life, read
My Brother Pier Giorgio: His Last Days, by Luciana Frassati
(New Hope Publications, 2002)

Finding Frassati

For an interview with Pier Giorgio's
niece Wanda Gawronska, watch
Sanctity Within Reach: Pier Giorgio Frassati (EWTN DVD)

Have just fifteen minutes to get to know him? Watch
Pier Giorgio Frassati: Get to Know Him (YouTube video)
https://www.youtube.com/watch?v=XaFLo36mYkA

Acknowledgments

This project stopped and started more times than I can recount. I'm grateful to everyone who encouraged me to continue and believed it would eventually materialize.

I owe a particular debt of gratitude to my sister Lisa Glowik, who often reminded me that it was not a matter of if but when. Olivia Zimberg got the ball rolling again. Olivia Spears skillfully charted its course and cheered its progress. My niece Amy Walsh helped clear away some key obstacles. A precious supporting cast of prayer and fasting warriors and patient listeners—especially Mother Louise Marie Flanigan, Ann Mayfield, Mary Pat Payne, Vince Phillips, Steve Smyth, Ramona Steltemeier, and Pam Zimberg—got it across the finish line. I am also most grateful to Bishop Philip Egan, who so kindly agreed to write the foreword. Celebrating Blessed Frassati's feast day with him in London in 2018 was a special highlight of my many years in ministry.

Finally, because of the generosity of each and every benefactor, past, present and future, and with the help of the Sister Servants of the Eternal Word, FrassatiUSA has been able to reach souls all around the world. With God's grace, together we will continue to introduce the spirituality of Blessed Pier Giorgio Frassati to a culture that so desperately needs Catholic models of courage,

Finding Frassati

true devotion to the Eucharist and Our Lady, and fidelity to the Church.

Beato Pier Giorgio Frassati, prega per noi.

—CMW
Nashville, Tennessee
April 23, 2021
Feast of St. George